Qbaloch99[1]

A SOUL'S CODE OF CONDUCT

JAMES L. CANNON

Abstract

Join Carter, Warden and Claire as they embark on a spiritual quest to discover a soul's code of morality, ethics, virtue and vice. It is your destiny, the great Archangel Michael has told them, to find and reveal for all humanity, the answers to the six epic questions:

1. WHAT IS THE MEANING OF HUMAN LIFE ON EARTH?
2. ARE HUMANS ETERNAL SOULS TRAPPED IN BODIES?
3. WHAT SPIRITUAL POWERS DO HUMANS POSSESS?
4. WHY IS THERE SUFFERING IN EVERY HUMAN LIFE?
5. **HOW SHOULD MODERN HUMAN SOULS LIVE?**
6. WHAT IS THE MEANING OF DEATH?

Each book in the series involves the answer to one of these questions with which they create a modern **Handbook of the Soul** containing fascinating insights into the meaning and purpose of human life, and most importantly what is expected of us while we are here.

Thousands of years of global philosophy, theology and science have been examined to find the credible purpose and meaning of human existence. Although the fictional stories surrounding it will entertain you, the handbook's real and rational answers to the timeless questions can help you see the true nature of your soul and the meaning of human life on earth.

Acclaim for the Series
Living as a Modern Soul in a Human Body

An author with an exceptional variety of life experiences has created an exciting series of short books addressing the fundamental questions of human existence.

Viewing life from the unique perspectives of a retired university vice president, a small city mayor, a corporate manager, an undercover intelligence operative, and a decorated military officer, Mr. Cannon provides a concise and thought-provoking account of the essential elements of wisdom necessary for us to thrive and grow.

The six stories, cover life's meaning, the keys to human happiness, and spiritual powers we can all claim, as well as the purpose of virtue, and morality. They also cover ways to encounter God, experience death and how to live well and die well.

The entertaining, six-book series--Living as a Modern Soul in a Human Body--was created to pass very practical and valuable, moral, ethical and spiritual knowledge to future generations. However, I heartily recommend the series as a great and easy read for anyone interested in becoming all they can be while on this Earth.

Jerry L. Beasley
President Emeritus
Concord University

Table of Contents

Book 5

A SOUL'S CODE OF CONDUCT

Introduction..1

Ch-1 Values of Life...3

Ch-2 Morality and Ethics...27

Ch-3 Virtue and Vice..45

Ch-4 The Pharaoh's Treasure 73

Ch-5 Attitude of the Soul..99

Appendix 1 Divine Standards...119

Appendix 2 Self-control..128

Author Biography..131

The six serial books in the series *Living as a Modern Soul in a Human Body* are best read in the following order:

Book 1. *The Meaning of Life*

Book 2. *Souls Trapped in Bodies*

Book 3. *Human Spiritual Powers*

Book 4. *Why Human Suffering*

Book 5. *A Soul's Code of Conduct*

Book 6. *The Meaning of Death*

A SOUL'S CODE OF CONDUCT

Book 5 in the Series

Living as a Modern Soul in a Human Body

JAMES L. CANNON

Copyright © 2000, 2023 by James L. Cannon

All rights reserved, except as permitted under the U.S. Copyright Act of 1976, no part of this publication may be reproduced, distributed or transmitted in any form or by any means, or stored in a database or retrieval system, without the prior written permission of the author.

Printed in the United States of America

ISBN-13: 978-0-9968528-8-3

Library of Congress Control Number: 2015915906

This book is dedicated to my grandsons
Zachary W. Moses
Landon C. Wright

Scriptural Verses from KJV

Cover design based on the Vitruvian Man of 1490
by Renaissance artist Leonardo da Vinci.

Introduction

This is the 5th book in a serial set of six books; this book covers the importance of good values, ways to develop spiritual moral and ethical conduct and the spiritual significance of virtue and vice. The book also covers the vital importance of your soul's attitude and how to manage it. This book is essential for those trying to understand the relationship between the soul within you and your outer human conduct.

The books in this series use a spiritual adventure story to convey vital spiritual truths. Those truths are outlined in the Handbook of the Soul section of each chapter.

For clarity, **important points and concepts** are **repeated** and **expanded** from chapter to chapter. The spiritual intelligence in the Handbook of the Soul is presented in a bulleted outline format of thought-sized bites for easier, reading. A glossary of significant terms as used in this set of stories is located at the end of the first book.

While acknowledging many and varied sources of information, it is the author who ultimately responsible for the content, and it is my earnest hope that these pages will help make life a little more meaningful for those whose eyes may chance upon them.

James L. Cannon
Soulsline9@gmail.com
8 October 2020

Spiritual power comes out of inward fellowship with God.
...E. Stanley Jones

[1] https://commons.wikimedia.org/wiki/File:Pasni_Balochistan_Desert_Night_Sky.jpg#filelinks. This file is licensed under the CreativeCommons Attribution-Share Alike 4.0 International license-

> Enter through the narrow gate.
> For wide is the gate and broad is the road that leads to destruction,
> and many enter through it.
> But small is the gate and narrow is the road that leads to life,
> and only a few find it.
>
> *Matthew 7:13,14*

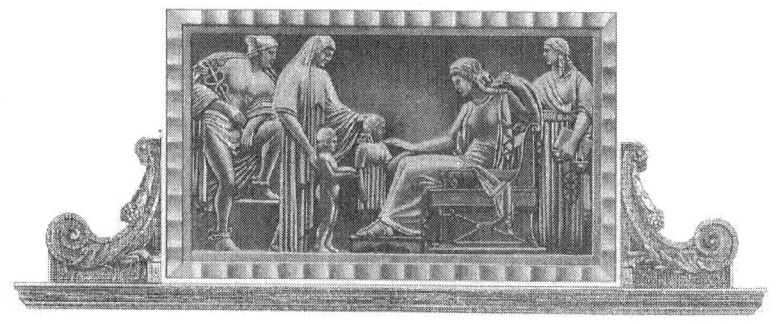

Chapter 1

<u>Values of Life</u>

Hi, Carter here; I am going to be speaking with you personally about this important section of our quest. It is now time to search for answers to the fifth great question of enduring importance to humanity:

HOW SHOULD MODERN HUMAN SOULS LIVE?

With Doc's medicine and my passionate prayers, God purged the evil of the bad drugs from my soul. I spent the next three years working to raise money for Doc's medical practice and establishing an online interactive network for him to help doctors all over the world.

The good doctor now travels only to participate in particularly difficult cases, but he is able to return to the base camp for months at a time to rest up while helping doctors and their patients through the online video practice.

I am still struggling with a few effects of that one illegal pill, but I am much healthier and far wiser. Doc, as he prefers to be called by his staff, has grown close to Warden and me, and he makes sure I do not forget my father's warnings about evil.

I relish our time together at the base camp; Doc, Warden, I and other members of the small staff spend a lot of time talking about the human soul and the meaning of life - subjects of interest to all.

> **"Enjoy the little things in life for some day you may look back and realize they were the big things."**
> *...Anonymous*

Chapter 1 Values of Life

I remember well my vision in the space capsule and the message that our souls progress through moral and ethical growth and by growing in virtue. So, for our journal, Warden and I research all we can find about values, morality and ethics while grandpa edits it.

Doc returns one time after a particularly vexing case, where an 18-year-old female patient would neither speak nor eat because she wanted to die. Both the girl's doctor and Doc knew he could save her with a natural cure he had used more than a dozen times with a high success rate.

There was every reason to believe her life could be saved, and that she could return to a normal life. However, the parents had a valid written medical power of attorney for their daughter. What made the case so difficult was the fact that the parents also wanted her to be allowed to die, saying only that the family had different values than the doctors.

Doc's herbal cure was not FDA approved; therefore, a judge ruled that it could not be used without the written consent of the patient or her parents.

The young woman's death troubled the doctors and nurses who watched her die. Doc knew Warden and I had done a lot of research on values, morality and ethics, so he asked me to do a seminar on values, which I present as follows:

Handbook of the Soul

The Values of Human Life

I. Preview

*Values are deeply held personal **beliefs and convictions** that help establish the basis of our sense of right and wrong.*

- *Our values represent the **activities** and **principles of behavior** that we respect, embrace and value most.*
- *We should each develop a personal code of values that will help govern our behavior.*
- *Our souls are **strengthened** by the **spiritual discipline required** for adopting and acting on **honorable values**.*

Fifty people in their eighties were asked what they would do differently if they could live their lives over.[1] Most said they would do the following:

1. *Take more risks*
2. *Do more things that would live on after they died*
3. *Reflect more about life while they were living it*

This suggests that in retrospect they might have put more value on being less fearful, and more value on doing some things more meaningful to leave a legacy in the wake of their lives.

Perhaps most importantly they would have put more value on the meaning and purpose of the lives they were leading as they lived out the days, months and years thereof.

The fact that there was so much consensus among them on these three things suggests we might want to do a little more of the same.

> Be careful where you spend your time and money for there you will find what you value most, and there you may find your soul as well.

Chapter 1 Values of Life

II. Introduction

I introduce the topic of values by recalling that for thousands of years, the wisest human beings have tried to answer many of life's fundamental questions like:

- *What is the purpose of life in a world filled with both good and evil?*
- *Is there a God and if so, what is the nature of God?*
- *What is the meaning of fate and death in human existence?*
- *What does it mean to live your life well?*

Bad Luck *- In other words, given the crazy circumstances of human existence, how do you go about living out your life in a way that will make you the best human being you can be? You must do so in spite of the uncertainties of fate, evil and the "slings and arrows of outrageous fortune" better known as bad luck and the other difficulties of life on earth.*

*What must we do, and how must we live to become the **best soul** we can be, instead of the **worst soul** we can be? And importantly, **how do we know the difference**?*

- ***In-not-of*** *- In ancient times, wise men concluded that we are on a journey in this world, but we are not of this world.*
- ***Ought to do*** *- By the end of the Middle Ages, the wisest among us were focused on what we ought to be doing on this journey and what we ought not to be doing.*
- ***Meaning*** *- In the last century onward, we have also tried to understand more about what is most meaningful in life and what matters most as we journey through our lives.*

These are the issues we will pursue in this chapter.

**Right is right, even if everyone is against it;
And wrong is wrong even if everyone is for it.**
...William Penn founder of Pennsylvania

Soul's Code of Conduct

<u>Noble Adventure</u> - *In many ways, human life can be understood as a grand and noble journey of adventure whereupon your spirit and soul come to earth in a human body. You are here to see how well you can surmount the challenges and temptations awaiting you in an often imperfect and unjust world.*

<u>Win the Game</u> - *If you want to "win the game" and make your life on earth count for as much as possible, you should learn to treat other people well and to develop a noble and virtuous character that is not so much centered on yourself.*

The following three points, are a preview of and a framework for the rest of this book.

1. <u>Your Values</u> - *When you have had enough experience in life to identify some values worth believing in, you should begin to establish the **values** that are important to you. For example, many people start out with values such as truth and friendship.*

2. <u>Code to Live By</u> - *The next step is to develop a personal code of right or wrong living that will govern your behavior according to your values. It can start out as a short list of the things you think you ought to do and the things you believe you ought not to do. For example, you may believe you should tell the truth about other people and that you should not steal from them.*

- **<u>Disordered Loves</u>** - *Our priorities are revealed by what we love, and God should be at the top of that list because he created us and he sustains us. A spiritual disorientation and disorder in life often results from our valuing and loving the wrong things.*

- **<u>Sense of Right</u> and <u>Wrong</u>** - *Abraham Lincoln envisioned the USA as a nation of self-governing equal citizens who were wise enough to be guided not just by self-interest or popular culture, but also by an enduring sense of right and wrong. What is the **enduring right and wrong** to which President Lincoln referred?*

How many legs does a dog have if you call the tail a leg?
Four, calling a tail a leg doesn't make it one.
.... *16th U.S. President Abraham Lincoln*

Chapter 1 Values of Life

- **Code of Ethics** - You may find that occasionally you have to agree to go by a certain accepted moral code of right or wrong behavior when you take a job or join some organizations. Such an **agreed upon** code of behavior is usually called a Code of Ethics.

3. Virtues - As you go through life, you should develop good moral and ethical habits called virtues. Virtues can help govern your conduct with good moral and ethical behavior that will eventually lead to improvement in your eternal character and the spiritual **transformation of your soul.** Such is the opportunity this life presents.

As a human being, you have this truly challenging **opportunity** to discover and follow the **highest values and virtues** and to mold and shape your soul according to them.

People unconsciously tend to adopt good and bad values from **family, media** and the **social culture**, so it is important to devote a little conscious time and attention to making sure you are getting it right.

The following are three keys to living a good and noble life:

1. *Self-Control*
2. *Faith*
3. *Virtue*

It is noted in the Wisdom of Solomon, that many people **devote** themselves **only** to the selfish pursuit of their **physical pleasures, passions** and **possessions. This stifles** even the **slightest inclination** toward divine wisdom and spiritual development.

We can enjoy physical pleasures and possessions as long as we know better than to devote our lives to them because they are not the purpose of our being.

"The reason a dog has so many friends
is that he wags his tail instead of his tongue."
...A. Lincoln

Soul's Code of Conduct

*We must develop values and a code of personal moral and ethical behavior powerful enough to guide us through ceaseless temptation in this immoral earthly society. A society on a treadmill of self-indulgence and in **hot pursuit** of many of the **wrong things**[2] such as fame, fortune, power and pleasure.*

*As we move along our journeys of life, we are being challenged to live an **unselfish, moral life of virtue, grace** and **honor** that will "ennoble our minds and elevate our souls."*

Let's explore how this might be done, and it begins with values.

III. <u>Values Defined</u>

*Values are deeply held personal **beliefs and convictions** that form the basis of your personal moral and ethical behavior. Your values represent the **activities and principles of human behavior** that you consciously or unconsciously respect, embrace and value most.*

1. <u>Person You Ought to Be</u> - *Your values or convictions and beliefs determine your standards of human decency and help anchor and govern your behavior. These values also help you make judgments about the kind of person you are and ought to be.*

2. <u>Internal Compass</u> - *Values can be defined also as principles upon which to base appropriate courses of action. Principles such as "Equal rights for all," "Excellence deserves admiration," and "People should be treated with respect and dignity."*

- *As such, a person's sense of right and wrong is based on that which they value as right or wrong.*

- *Personal values provide an internal reference for what is good, beneficial, important, useful, beautiful and desirable.*

"Do not value money for any more nor any less than it's worth;
it is a good servant but a bad master."
...Alexandre Dumas fils, Camille

Chapter 1 Values of Life

3. <u>Admirable</u> or <u>Self-Serving</u> - There are admirable values like truth, courage and fairness or more self-serving, selfish values like pleasure, power and fame. In a way, your values form guidelines for your conscience, and they help you decide what is right and what is wrong in most situations.

Values should also help you decide that, which is most worth doing in the valuable time you are being given here on earth. Our values and principles should **inspire us** to live our lives and pursue our destinies in a way that will leave the world a better place than we found it.

- **<u>Stand for Something</u>** - U.S. founding father Alexander Hamilton said, "You must stand for something or you will fall for anything." Your values are what you stand for.

- **<u>Lost in the Woods</u>** - Having no values in life, would be like being lost in the woods with no map and no compass: you would have a hard time figuring out which way to go. Without solid values and your own code of ethics, you are spiritually disoriented (lacking direction).

- **<u>Dependent on Others</u>** - Being spiritually disoriented makes you more dependent for direction on others. They may lead you astray at the many forks in the road of life where temptation is greatest, and where you must often make the most difficult and important choices.

- **<u>Value of Nothing</u>** - There is growing concern that we are becoming a materialistic society, concerned about the price of all things, but the value of nothing.

4. <u>You Become Your Values</u> - When you practice the values, virtues or vices you believe in, they become a part of the character of your immortal spirit, and they shape the nature and eternal destiny of your soul.

> **Values are like fingerprints. Nobody's are exactly the same, but you leave traces of them all over everything you do.**
> *...Renowned Performer Elvis Presley*

Soul's Code of Conduct

The values you adopt as your own will also affect your attitude toward life on earth and your responses or reactions to the experiences you encounter throughout your life's journey.

IV. Sources of Values

1. Ancient Greeks - *So, where do our values come from? Among the earliest written records of human values and beliefs concerning the origins of good and evil are the philosophical writings of the ancient Greeks. They were very interested in the concept of good values, character and good citizenship.*

- **Displeasure of the Gods** - *In the earliest years of their civilization, the ancient Greeks assumed that the problems and evil in their lives were the result of the displeasure of their gods and goddesses and the random actions of fate.*

- **Souls of the Citizens** - *Eventually their greatest thinkers like Socrates, Plato and Aristotle began to understand that the source of good and evil in human affairs was more often rooted in the souls of the citizens themselves.*

- **Unbridled Passion** - *The philosophers discovered that the unbridled human passions like anger, greed, jealousy, lust, hatred and selfishness etc. were the real sources of disorder and discontent in the lives of the Greek people. The solution to these problems requires learning to control unbridled passion and selfish desire with self-control and virtuous habits.*

2. Scriptural Teaching - *Other sources of important values are our scriptural traditions that have taught us the values of*

- Faith
- Hope
- Love of God and neighbor

**Hope is a compound of desire, expectation, patience and joy.
And as such, it is the indispensable medicine of the soul.**
...Ralph W. Sockman

Chapter 1 Values of Life

*The **Ten Commandments** of Mosaic Law embody the following values:*

- *Value of Truth- shall not lie*
- *Value of Marriage – shall not cheat on spouse*
- *Value of God - one God, no idols, swear not in God's name, keep Sabbath holy*
- *Value of Parents – honor father and mother*
- *Value of Life - shall not murder*
- *Value of Honesty – shall not steal*
- *Value of Contentment – shall not yearn for(covet) property of others*

*The wonderful **opportunities** or the bad **problems** in **your life** are often the **result** of the following:*

- *Values you hold dear*
- *Choices you make*
- *Actions you take*
- *Friends you make*

As a child, you likely adopt initial values from your family. Over time, initial values will be strengthened, altered or replaced as you consciously and subconsciously adopt good or bad values from media, religion, school, friends, books, movies, music, popular culture and other sources of influence.

Friends, especially good friends, have a great deal of influence on one another, so be very careful about the character of those whom you choose as your friends for they will definitely have some influence on your character.

It is important to be aware of the fact that your values can be affected by so many negative influences, especially during your first 25 or so years on the planet.

> **"Surround yourself
> with people who are going to lift you higher."**
> *...Opra Winfrey*

According to Scholar Morris Massey, values are formed during the following three approximate periods:
1. **Imprint** period from birth to 7 years
2. **Modeling** period from 8 – 13 years; copying family, friends and media
3. **Socialization** period from 14 – 21 years; result of media, friends, family, personal experience, education and other influential people.

As bedrock convictions and beliefs, values once established are not easily changed; however, over time with exposure to different influences your values can be altered. Your moral and ethical behavior is based on your values and is usually consistent with them.

The culture of a society is based, in part, on the public expression of common personal values that groups of people find important in their day-to-day lives. These shared values lay the foundations of a society's laws, customs and traditions.

V. Honorable Core Values

A good set of values should include honorable **core values of universal moral truths**[3] that have the most influence on the way you act, along with a number of other secondary values that influence your behavior in specific situations.

Expect to Abide - If you don't already own them, you should consider adopting as many of the following generally accepted, honorable core values as possible. They are very important values that are widely respected by most decent human beings across most modern human cultures, and good people everywhere will expect you to abide by them.

Our souls are **strengthened** by the **spiritual discipline required** for adopting and acting on **honorable values**.

"Bad company corrupts good character."
1st Corinthians 15:33

Chapter 1 Values of Life

The following are 24 honorable core values many people possess or would like to own:

1. Truth... Most people respect the truth, and they also respect those who tell the truth in spite of the temptations to lie or exaggerate. Truth is a beautiful and powerful virtue that must be respected and revered. To disrespect truth is to degrade your own character.

- **Distrust** - Trustworthiness and personal integrity are based on truth and honesty. Few people care for those they cannot trust. Lying is a violation of both body and spirit because the human energy system identifies lies as poison.

- **Maturity or Brainwashing** - We mature in our beliefs step by step, experience after experience. As we mature, we may encounter circumstances that cause us to change our beliefs and thereby come closer to understanding the truth of reality. However, we must be sure we are not being brainwashed into exchanging true beliefs for false ones.

- **Lie of Life** - Without truth, your life becomes a big lie with little basis in reality and no certainty or real meaning. As the esteemed philosopher Aristotle once said, "A goal of truth is to conform your mind to the way things are."

- **Spiritual Discipline** - The ultimate **purpose** of seeking truth is not just accurate information.
    - Part of the transformation of your soul takes place through the difficult and purifying process of rejecting dishonesty, exaggeration and self-serving lies.
    - As you learn to seek and speak the truth in your life, your soul becomes **strengthened by the spiritual discipline required for being honest.**

2. Courage...Courage is not just a trait that makes wartime heroes. Having courage is having the fortitude and strength of character to maintain faith, hope, joy, cheerfulness and optimism in spite of negative people, difficult situations or challenging circumstances.

- **Moan, Whine** - *No one wants to hear you moan, whine and complain just because you lack the strength of character or the* **courage to face difficulty with a positive attitude**.

- **Fear** - *Having courage is also being brave enough to speak the truth even if it makes you look bad. Courage is not a lack of fear; it is the inner strength to control your fear before it controls your actions; it is the decision to override the powerful emotion of fear that may be welling up in your soul.*

- **Quiet Roar** - *According to Mary Anne Radmacher, courage doesn't always roar. Sometimes it is the quiet voice at the end of the day saying I will try again tomorrow.*

- **Stronger Soul** - *Courage is the virtue of fortitude applied to everyday life; it is withstanding adversity when it comes against us and "not letting it rob us of our ability to create or act."*[4]

- **Doing Right Despite** - *Courage is about doing what wisdom tells you is right despite adversity, challenges, and threats to your own wellbeing. The result being to leave your soul stronger for having been courageous. After all, you have been given this life because you are strong enough to live it.*[5]

3. Justice and Fairness....Justice is equal accountability before the law. Fairness equates to a sense of fair play and the expectation that you will go by whatever rules are involved, that the laws and rules should apply equally to everyone regardless of status, creed or race.

- *You should honor your word always. You must stand behind your signature on a contract or ruin your reputation.*

- *Your debts should be paid according to their terms, or you default against your character as well as the lender.*

- *When responsible for others, you should treat them all as you would like to be treated, in accordance with the laws, policies and circumstances in force at the time.*

"A boy doesn't have to go to war to be a hero; he can say
he doesn't like pie when he sees there isn't enough to go around."
...Edgar Watson Howe

Chapter 1 Values of Life

- In social situations, you must be careful not to gossip or speak ill of others behind their backs or make fun at their expense.

4. Unselfishness...means getting over yourself, getting your focus off your own needs and onto those of others. You are not here just to pleasure yourself but to build your eternal character by thinking about others, helping others and generally becoming others minded. In all things, become more a giver and less a taker.

- **Friends** - According to Dale Carnegie, you can make more friends in two months by becoming interested in other people than you can in two years by trying to get other people interested in you.
- Show an **interest** in them and **ask** about other people's lives, jobs, dreams and kids, pets or hobbies.
- **Trap** - Selfishness is one of the hardest spiritual traps from which to escape.

5. Love... is not just an emotion; it is a **commitment** and encouragement to friends, sweethearts and family. Your love should be an action verb moving you to act. To be in a personal relationship of love is to share control and put another's desires in line with your own. Love is the **commitment** to meet other people's needs. Emotion or feeling are only its symptoms.

- Love consists of commitment, benevolence, action, resilience and volition.
- It is **benevolent**, meaning it brings a powerful attitude of goodness toward someone and wanting always the best for them.
- It is an **action**-oriented commitment involving all kinds of activity in support of the loved one.
- That love is **resilient**, means it can withstand all kinds of difficulties and disagreements without giving up on the one who is loved.

Soul's Code of Conduct

- Such a commitment takes an **act of will power** to truly love someone that much, which means it is an act of choice.

6. Duty... hard work, strong work ethic, moderation, self-discipline and self-improvement are the values that help make us strong and prosperous. – "If a man works not, he ought not eat."[6]

7. Thrift... is efficiency in the production and consumption of all resources.

8. Humility... is a true precondition for the spiritual transformation of your soul. It is not thinking less of yourself, just thinking of yourself less often.

- Humility is the master of pride, and it willingly accepts responsibility for moral faults, human flaws and wrongdoing.
- Humility chooses a kind response to criticism and is graceful and patient with all.
- Self-importance and hypocrisy are replaced with authenticity, as we are concerned less often about ourselves.
- According to theologian Charles Swindol, excess pride is an insidious disease of the soul, so we should avoid thinking more of ourselves than we ought.[7]

Mia noted that these seem to be the kind of values you would expect great people to have, and certainly they are the values of people you would respect. Casey added that they are the kinds of values you would want to encourage in your children. Doc said they are the core values each good person should aspire to owning.

9. Self-control...is discipline, moderation, restraint, politeness and patience. Equanimity is calm levelheaded self-control and composure. As noted elsewhere, self-control is the door to heaven.[8]

> "Alas, I know if I ever became truly humble, I would be proud of it."
> ...Ben Franklin

Chapter 1 Values of Life

***10. Freedom**...is independence of thought and action, liberty, the pursuit of happiness. Each person is to have an equal right to the most extensive basic liberty that is compatible with a similar liberty for others.[9] Or in the immortal words of Theodore Roosevelt, "The freedom to swing your fist ends where my nose begins."*

***11. Goodness**...is righteousness, Godliness, a feeling of being clean down through your soul.*

***12. Wisdom**...is the ability to use information and knowledge effectively to make important decisions, to use prudence to think through your actions before taking them and to learn from your mistakes.*

***13. Sanctity of Life**...is belief that all life is precious and that murder, abortion or suicide is generally wrong.*

***14. Physical Health & Fitness**...people everywhere usually admire those with the discipline to stay fit and honor the bodies they have been given.*

***15. Moderation**...moderation or temperance is the avoidance of excess or deficiency in human behavior.*

***16. Equality**...all people are not honorable nor of equal character nor of equal ability. But all humans are considered to be equally valuable.*

***17. Beauty**...beauty is the appealing expression of life's most attractive features to offset the harsher experience of life's difficulty.*

***18. Kindness**...is charity, respect, civility, sympathy, empathy and benevolence; caring for others and concern for their well-being and acting to promote their success. Kindness requires that we learn to empathize with others, even though as children we are by nature self-centered.[10]*

***19. Creativity**... the ability to make something new, beautiful or useful.*

***20. Prudence**...is considering the consequences of your actions before you take them.*

***21. Peace**...as opposed to conflict and strife. Peace of mind includes a feeling that all is well in your world.*

People are what they believe, think and do.
...Author Anton Chekhov

22. Trustworthiness...*is a broad value concerned with all the qualities and behaviors that make a person worthy of trust, especially integrity, honesty, promise keeping and loyalty*

23. Responsibility... *responsibility speaks to the moral obligations to be accountable, pursue excellence and exercise self-restraint.*

24. Citizenship...*includes civic virtues and duties that prescribe how we ought to behave as part of a community.*

- *Good citizenship is doing one's share to make society work in the present and for future generations.*
- *A good citizen works hard and smart, respects the law, reports crimes, serves on juries, becomes knowledgeable about national issues and votes responsibly, pays taxes and protects the environment.*

VI. Table of Values and Priorities

Carter continued his presentation with the table on the next page that lists many of the things that human being's value. You can use this list to help you identify the priorities in your life and the values you hold most dear by considering the **way you spend your time, money and attention**.

- *You could reflect for a while on the things that are important to you at this point in your life.*
- *Use the table as your own; delete values you consider unimportant and add others until you have a pretty good table of what is important to you.*
- *Identify the ten values you consider most important.*
- *The next step is to rank those you identified from 1 through 10 making 1 the most important and 10 the least important.*
- *Finally, you can rank each of the other values on a scale of 1 to 10 to see which you value highly. You must be honest with yourself if this exercise is to be of any use to you.*

Chapter 1 Values of Life

Table of Human Values and Priorities

Achievement	Gambling & risk taking	Peace of mind
Adventure	Great Car	Physical beauty
Ambition	Generosity	Leadership position
Altruism[11]	Glory	Physical Possessions
Appreciation	Godliness	Pleasure
Art	Good Education	Power
Beauty	Good Health	Privacy
Being "cool"	Good Job	Prudence
Benevolence	Good Marriage	Recognition
Charity	Goodness	Respect
Citizenship	Helping Other People	Relationship with God
Children	Hobbies	Righteousness
Compassion	Happiness	Romance
Control (of others)	Honesty	Safety and Security
Self-control	Honor	Sanctity of Life
Concern for Others	Humility	Sensual Pleasures
Contentment	Intelligence	Good food & drink
Courage	Justice	Drinking Alcohol
Creativity	Kindness	Getting high
Discipline	Leisure	Pornography & Lust

Soul's Code of Conduct

Efficiency	Long Life	Sincerity
Enjoyment	Love	Spirituality
Entertainment	Meaningful Work	Sports
Equality	Nice House	Strong Talent
Faith	Nice clothes	Strong Work Ethic
Fairness	Nice possessions	Temperance
Fame	Peaceful relationships	Thrift
Family	Entertainment:	Truth
Financial Security	Dancing	Travel
Fortune	Listening to music	Wealth
Freedom	Reading	Wildlife
Friendship	Watching TV	Winning
Fun	Watching movies	Wisdom
Fulfilling Sex Life	Other entertainment	Worldly Success

At the time of this writing, there is an excellent and more complete list of values and their meanings at www.values.com. Try not to indicate the things **you think you ought** to value most. Try instead to determine your true priorities at this stage of your life, based on the way you spend your **time, money and attention**.

It might be useful to compare the things you think you **should** value most with the things you **do** value most.

Chapter 1 Values of Life

We become closer to God by the spiritual discipline of a virtuous life. With virtue comes wisdom. In a process called sanctification, you and God reform your character to reflect the values of His will for the best your soul can become in light of all eternity. In modern culture, the choice to honor Divine values might encounter all kinds of opposition and ridicule.[12]

Let not kindness and truth leave you.
...Proverbs 3:1-4

Vatican 1,000 Lire coin God cradling man

Avoiding Temptation

The best way to deal with temptation is to avoid it altogether. It is much easier to deal with a door than it is to overcome an attractive temptation. We must keep away from the doors that lead to the temptations, for instance those fighting prostitution should stay out of the places where prostitutes are located. Those fighting gluttony should avoid the refrigerator door.

VII. Summary

*Values are deeply held personal **beliefs and convictions** that form the basis of your sense of right and wrong and help establish the things you care about most.*

- *Our values represent the **activities** and **principles of behavior** that we respect, embrace and value most.*

- *We should each develop a personal code of moral living that will govern our behavior according to honorable **values** and try to mold and shape our souls according to those values.*

- *Our souls are **strengthened** by the **spiritual discipline required** for adopting and acting on **honorable values** such as the following widely held scriptural values:*

  ✓ *Put Nothing Ahead of a Sacred Relationship with God*

  ✓ *Use Not the Name of God in Vain*

  ✓ *The Sabbath Day Keep Holy*

  ✓ *Love Closely and Respect Your Parents and Children*

  ✓ *Kill Not Human Beings*

  ✓ *Do Not Commit Adultery*

  ✓ *Steal Not*

  ✓ *Lie Not to or About Other People*

  ✓ *Seek Not More Than You Are Due*

For more on examples of enduring human values please consult the appendix.

Carter with you still, and thank you for participating in the presentation on values. I hope you found it worthwhile.

Chapter 1 Values of Life

Doc says that Warden and I seem to have a talent for making complex things clearer and simpler, and he asks Warden to give the next presentation on Morality and Ethics, which should be excellent.

We may have lost APOLLYON for good; their organization deteriorated from internal corruption, and then became part of the new Socialist government and hopefully forgot about us.

During the past 20 years the country lost its values of Freedom, Democracy and Free Market Capitalism. The people were lured into the deceptive economic vice of Socialism where the government takes over businesses and corporations and supposedly becomes responsible for everyone instead of everyone being free and responsible for themselves.

Even though there is ample evidence that Socialism and Communism wreck economies, the liberal politicians make it sound so good with social justice, economic equality for all, loads of free government services, free college, free healthcare, free housing, and free food and clothing for the needy all to be paid for by taxing the rich and printing money if necessary.

They said there would be jobs for everyone in a glorious workers paradise. It looks like they promised everything to gain political power and it worked except that we now have the opposite of a paradise.

The Socialist administration has taken over most corporations in the name of the people. Those who still work in them say they are driving them into bankruptcy with wasteful mismanagement and corruption. Evidently, they are filling the upper management positions with socialist political cronies with no experience in business management.

Why then would some politicians advocate a failed economic system? Because it is a path to power that will leave them in control of the country. Once in control they can amass, through corruption, as much personal wealth as they want, while driving everyone else into poverty.

The Socialist administration is also seizing peoples' investments and property to make everyone economically equal. Except that the government officials are keeping a healthy share of what they take for themselves. Small businesses are closing and their owners are fleeing the country due to super high taxes and socialist edicts and regulations.

Soul's Code of Conduct

Aspire to High and Holy Values

It seems that the economy is gradually failing, and half the people have lost their jobs. Most have been put into meaningless work camps to keep them busy while they live on government welfare.

We are all worrying about our families, but there seems to be little anyone can do with the government now controlling so much of our lives. Here at the base camp, we are staying positive and praying for better times.

It is hard to imagine how we allowed socialism to take root in our society when there are, for all to see, so many examples of failed socialist and communist economies in other countries. The problem is you can now go from kindergarten to college graduation and without ever having to study economics or economic history.

Furthermore, the news media has shifted so far left that most reporters don't understand economics and don't report on anything but the need for more socialism and communism to address so called "social justice" issues of inequality where equal opportunity is no longer enough.

Radical redistribution of wealth from those who earn it to those who don't is the new economic objective.

Chapter 1 Values of Life

In addition, there has been massive voter fraud from uncontrolled mail-in ballots, and voting without proof of identity, which has allowed multiple votes by the same people many of whom are illegal aliens or citizens who have been dead for years. This allowed the left to claim victory in highly questionable elections all across the country.

Also, extensive vote harvesting has been proven where older or indigent people have been paid to let someone else fill out their ballots. Meanwhile in every state, truckloads of legitimate mail in ballots for conservative candidates have been found after the elections in dumpsters and landfills. Despite the evidence, liberal judges, governors and legislatures have managed to block effective reform.

The eventual result of the growing economic ignorance and election fraud was the rigged "election" of the socialist government under which we now suffer.

The negative culture is like a rushing river trying to drag us along with it. Living honorably is like swimming upstream against the current. However, an elite core of individuals will we be, who by doing so shall build the spiritual muscle and stamina to prepare us for a nobler way and a better day.

---

[1] Bob Welch, 52 lessons from A Christmas Carol, Thomas Nelson, Nashville, 2015, p55

[2] Charles Swindol, *A Life Well Lived,* Thomas Nelson, Nashville, TN, p.xv

[3] Michael Josephson enunciated six pillars of character

[4] The Great Courses, Fears, J Rufus, *Life lessons from the Great Books*, Guidebook p.125

[5] Sam Timm, Wildwings.com, wrapped canvas art, item # F874722696

[6] Holy Bible, 2nd Thessalonians 3:10, King James Version

[7] Charles Swindol, *A Life Well Lived*, Thomas Nelson, Nashville, TN, p.84

[8] C.S. Lewis, *Mere Christianity,* Harper Collins, San Francisco, CA p.103

[9] Grim, *Questions of Value*, Guidebook Part 2 p.13, The Great Courses

[10] Charles Swindol, *A Life Well Lived*, p35-36

[11] Altruism is acting to promote someone else's welfare, even at some risk or cost to ourselves

[12] Charles Swindol, *The Owner's Manual for Christians*, Thomas Nelson, Nashville, 2009, p.157

Chapter 2

<u>Morality and Ethics</u>

Hello, I am Warden and it is my pleasure to invite you to sit in on our seminar. Doc asked me to do a seminar on Morality and Ethics, so with the full staff at the base camp, Doc has turned things over to me.

To bring you up to speed, I had started out by asking the staff if they knew exactly what morality means, what ethics means and the difference between the two terms. This led to a discussion about why they are so important to start with from both a spiritual and a practical point of view.

I explained that it had been spiritually impressed upon Carter that **it was through values, morality, ethics and virtue that the human soul progresses.** Therefore, Carter and I did a great deal of research into these concepts.

The practical importance of morality and ethics is that the benefits of civilization would not be possible without a generally agreed upon code of behavior that allowed people to trust one another to a certain extent. For instance, we usually assume that people are telling the truth at least until we have reason to believe otherwise.

Good words are worth much and cost little.
...George Herbert

Chapter 2 Morality and Ethics

Without that one moral and ethical assumption alone, it would make doing business, traveling, buying, investing and many other important aspects of human activity much more difficult if not impossible. One of the staff said the criminal elements of society tend to be unethical and immoral, which is probably why they are criminals.

It was generally agreed that most people could be trusted to tell the truth except in situations where the temptation for them to benefit from lying might be greater than their desire to be honest.

Doc said, "It is up to each society to encourage in their people a strong sense of obligation to follow the society's moral and ethical customs, and it's up to each individual to do so. This builds trust in communities that is very important in modern civilization where we are dependent on honest relations with other people for most of the goods and services we utilize."

Everyone pitched in with examples like, if we could not trust our doctors; they might tell us we need unnecessary treatments or surgeries just so they could make more money. If we could not trust the banks to protect our money, people to prepare food safely, our spouses to be faithful, our neighbors not to steal from us, or our employers not to cheat us life would be much, much more difficult.

We would have to spend so much time checking up on everything and everyone that there would be little time or peace of mind with which to enjoy life. Even Charles Darwin claimed that it is precisely morality that distinguishes humans from other animals.[1]

After a great warm up discussion about the practical importance of morality and ethics, I am ready to present the following information as Carter and I have it written in our "Handbook of the Soul."

**Human worth is in the weight of our souls
not in the value of our bank accounts.**
...Tony Robbins

Soul's Code of Conduct

Handbook of the Soul
Morality & Ethics

I. Preview

The **good** or **evil in your life** is often the **result** of the **values you hold, the thoughts you think, the choices you make, the actions you take** and the **friends you make**. You ought to develop a moral code for personal behavior that is based on self-control and good core values.

II. Morality

In the last chapter, we discussed the importance of having good values on which to base your life. While values refer to your personal belief system and its convictions and priorities, morality refers to **conduct** that is right or wrong in your personal behavior. Usually, our conduct is based on our values.

The Encarta dictionary defines morality as standards of conduct that are generally accepted as right or proper. Morality is also defined as **motivation based on ideas of right and wrong.**

Your personal **code of morality** determines how you conduct yourself when moral questions of right, honorable or wrong behavior toward other people arise in your private life.

Chapter 2 Morality and Ethics

*Therefore, living a moral life means living according to a set of ideals regarding what is right and ought to be done, versus what is wrong and ought not to be done. It covers a few private activities such as how well you **control your passions** for the sensory pleasures of life. However, it mostly applies to the way **you treat and interact** with other people.*

For example, moral behavior would mean being unselfish with others, by being there for your friends when they need you, by telling the truth even if it makes you look bad or by maintaining your higher standards of sexual behavior when under pressure to give in.

Your personal morals determine the ways you interact with other people regarding the following kinds of behavior:

- *prudent or indecent behavior*
- *good or bad behavior*
- *moderate or excessive behavior*

Human beings should be developing behavior that meets at least the known divine and enduring standards of right and wrong. For example, it is morally correct for you to do the following, and it is morally wrong or immoral not to do so:

- *To provide love and care for your family if you have one*
- *To show reverence toward your parents*
- *To control your temper and restrain anger*
- *To restrain your desires and appetites for excess alcoholic drink or too much food*
- *To deter temptations for tobacco, illegal drugs and illicit sex*
- *To be honest, unselfish and just in your dealings with other people*
- *To accept personal responsibility for living and acting honorably as a respectable member of the human race*

Soul's Code of Conduct

*Doing the following makes a big difference in whom you are and **whom you become**:*

- *Staying **positive** and accepting your share of the pain, difficulty and misfortune of life with courage and forbearance instead of constantly whining and complaining*

- *Standing with the **good against the bad** and inspiring others to do the same*

- *Helping and **encouraging** other people who may be in legitimate need of assistance*

- *Putting your family, your friends or your country's interest thoughtfully at the center of your attention and action sometimes even ahead of your own interests and desires[2]*

- *If you are a person of faith, honoring God by living with an **attitude of thanksgiving**, unselfish humility, joy, faith and optimism*

Life's Greatest Challenge - Morality includes doing your very best to do the moderate, sensible, right, just and unselfish things with your limited time and energy. Living a moral life means not falling in to a shallow, **self-serving life style** with a lust for the sensory pleasures of a sordidly ordered soul.

Do not expect it will be easy to overcome all these temptations. Withstanding the continuous lures of selfishness, pride, anger, envy, gluttony, greed, laziness and a lust for illegitimate pleasures has been and is **life's greatest challenge** for all of humanity.

- *These are the kinds of **temptations that truly test and try our souls.***

- *The desire to win in competition must not overcome honest ethical conduct and playing by the rules.*

- *It is better to be an honest, gracious loser than a pompous, prideful victor who is willing to cheat to win.*

Chapter 2 Morality and Ethics

Inner Strength - *Developing the inner strength to overcome such temptations is among the central challenges of our human existence because our moral behavior appears to be one of the **decisive determinants** of our eternal destiny.*

We should feel honor bound to act with honesty and integrity within all our relationships including the following:

- *Marriage*
- *Friendship*
- *Business*
- *Employment*
- *Citizenship*

Contaminating Our Energy - *Violating our honor or compromising our integrity is said to contaminate the energy of our souls and eventually to undermine our physical health.*[3]

Morality is sometimes defined as the human ability to judge the right or wrong of our own actions. 18th century Bishop Joseph Butler defined conscience as the voice of God within our spirit. A voice that judges our conduct and often urges us to stop and think about what we are doing.

If you are not sure what to do in a difficult moral situation, pray for guidance, listen to your conscience or follow the golden rule by treating other people, as you would like to be treated.

Morally correct behavior in your interactions with other people will test some of your most important character traits and values. It will include your standards of human decency, your degree of selfishness or unselfishness and the general goodness, decency and honor of your spirit.

> "We can really respect a man
> only if he doesn't always look out for himself first."
> ...Johann Wolfgang von Goethe, German novelist

Soul's Code of Conduct

Moral Strength - Your moral strength is your degree of resistance to immoral temptation. It involves both knowing the right thing to do and **overcoming the temptation** to do the wrong thing.

Moral strength is the ability to carry through and do what is right **even when it hurts** and even when **no one else is looking!**

When humans are tempted to irritability or anger, but by great effort overcome the selfish tendency and act instead from the spirit of patience and calm, then in that moment have they practiced a degree of self-conquest. In so doing have they also strengthened, by degree, the power in their souls.

Your actions with regard to small issues of right or wrong makes a difference in your moral strength, and they can help prepare you for the bigger moral challenges to come.

Flourishing - Thousands of years ago, the great philosopher Aristotle observed that for human beings to flourish and be happy in this life they need possess but the following four things:

1. Virtuous character
2. Wisdom
3. Moral strength (to do what is right even when it hurts)
4. Friendships (and a social connectedness to others)

Moral and ethical obligations arise from the fact that humans should have an unselfish spirit of cooperation because we benefit from helping one another and living in right relationship to one another.

Constructive Harmony - This requires us to behave in ways that make it possible to live together in constructive harmony without antagonizing those with whom we must live.

- A person of good character acknowledges civic responsibilities, desires to contribute to the overall public good and treats others honorably.

Chapter 2 Morality and Ethics

- *Responsible citizenship involves doing one's share as a member of a community. It embodies both civic duties and moral and ethical virtues.*

Previously, we have talked about how we become the individuals we are, based on the **values we hold,** the thoughts we think, **the choices we make, the actions we take** and the **friends we make**.

You can actually choose the kind of person you want to be and then intentionally do what it takes to become that kind of person. For instance, whenever you are faced with a moral choice, ask yourself if you are willing to become the kind of person that makes the bad, selfish choices; if not, you must make the right choices.

For example, I recently made a purchase at a store, and when I got back to my car to unload the shopping cart, I found that a couple of small items had fallen under a rug in the cart, and that I hadn't paid for them.

My feet hurt, I was tired, it was hot and I was parked quite a long way from the store. I really did not want to go all the way back in the store to pay the small price of the items. I rationalized that it had been an accident and besides they cost less than a dollar each, so it would be no big loss to the store.

I started to go on home when I realized that I would rather be the kind of person that would go back and pay for the items than the kind of person who would not. I recognized that **my actions would actually help determine which kind of person I became.** Therefore, I thought about whom I wanted to become then went back and paid for the items. I felt very good about my choice, and my feet even quit hurting.

III. <u>Ethics</u>

*The terms morality and ethics refer to right and wrong conduct, and they are often used interchangeably. However, ethics is more concerned with following **agreed upon** standards of right or wrong conduct.*[4]

Whereas your personal moral code is between you and God, you must adhere to the existing ethical standards where you work or there are likely to be consequences. For instance, you could be fired for cheating customers or coworkers or for stealing company property.

Soul's Code of Conduct

Ethics often refers to standards governing the conduct of members of a profession such as doctors, lawyers or dentists. There are three aspects to ethics:[5]

- *Discerning right from wrong*
- *Committing to do what is right*
- *Doing what is right*

Why are ethics important?[6]

- *Clients, customers and patients must be able to* **trust** *the professionals they seek help from to treat them honestly and fairly.*
- *It is very important in business and professional relationships that we not cheat or deceive other people.*
- *There is an inner benefit to knowing that, even when it is difficult, you have the power to do the fair, just and honorable thing. And doing so preserves your reputation as a good person with whom to do business.*
- *Any great business will be quickly destroyed if it earns a reputation for dishonesty.*

The term ethics, as opposed to morality, is frequently used more in reference to your conduct at work or matters of money or issues involving fairness and playing by rules and professional standards. Ethical behavior involves obeying laws and following rules so as not to cheat or disadvantage other people.

Codes of Ethics - *Some employers have written codes of ethics in employee handbooks, which in some cases employees must read and sign as a condition of employment or membership in an organization.*

Professional associations or licensing boards usually have a written code of ethics to which their members must agree. Lawsuits have been won because members of a profession violated the ethical code and cheated a customer.

Chapter 2 Morality and Ethics

Mostly, however, ethical behavior involves following a code of conduct based on society's generally accepted standards of moral and ethical decency covering what is right and wrong in most situations.

The unwritten code includes an understanding of the personal behaviors that are permitted and forbidden in the proper conduct of social relationships and employment.

*There are also interpersonal issues that may not get you fired, but may cause other people to avoid you and **distrust** you. If, for example, you lack virtue and exaggerate, gossip or spread rumors about other people or if you blame others for your failures and don't follow the rules of common courtesy.*

Ethics, as agreed upon guidelines of right and wrong conduct can help you cope with the many varied challenges, temptations and difficult choices in life.

- *One guiding moral principle is moderation known as the **golden mean**. This hallowed maxim warns against going too far to **excess** on one hand or not doing enough and **insufficiency** on the other hand.*
- *A famous guiding principle from religion is the **golden rule** of doing unto others, as you would have them do unto you.*
- *The **Platinum rule** in business is to do for your customers what they want you to do.*

*Ethics is technically a pre-agreed upon approach to morality with **wisdom** consisting of knowing which of the right guiding principles to apply to the situation at hand.*

These guiding principles are found in wisdom literature such as religious works as well as in many of the writings of famous philosophers.

<u>Fair and Honest</u> - *The simplest and most **basic principle of ethics** is to be fair and honest with others, especially in the realm of business, sports or other forms of competition.*

Soul's Code of Conduct

This requires an understanding of what is fair and right or wrong in differing situations. This is where your values and written codes of ethics come in to play helping you make accurate judgments about what is just, fair, right or wrong.

- As our society has become multi-cultural, the values and moral standards are a little less consistent.
- It can be a little more difficult to sustain **agreed upon** standards of moral and ethical conduct that form the basis of social ethics.

*Unfortunately, there is no comprehensive, widely agreed upon, written **list** of these guiding ethical principles, so you have to pick them up as you go through life or seek them out through various religious lessons and texts or dedicated research into morality and ethics.*

*Hopefully, your values and personal code of moral standards will be as good as, or better than the **ethical standards** you are expected to follow at work and as a citizen in society at large.*

The following are some examples of unethical behavior in the workplace:

1. Lying to or about other people
2. Falsifying reports or documents
3. Stealing the work, possessions or ideas of others
4. Taking credit for things you have not done
5. Falsely accusing others
6. Stealing company supplies, materials, ideas, information or products
7. Withholding important information or testimony

All the ways of a man are right in his own eyes.
...Proverbs 21:2

8. *Not adhering to confidentiality agreements, contracts or obligations*

9. *Spreading damaging gossip about your company, its employees or competitors*

10. *Undermining your company; intentionally withholding effort or aiding competitors*

11. *Doing less than your best at what you are being paid to do*

Honest Competition - *In our world, business, sports, politics and other things must be conducted on a fair and sincere basis of honest competition without fraud or deception. Anything dishonest or unfair would be unethical and maybe illegal. Therefore, we must understand the importance of ethics as the character-building part of the rulebook.*

Sense of Fairness - *Ethically correct behavior in your dealings with other people will test some of your most important character traits and values such as your honesty, integrity and your sense of fairness.*

- *You must establish self-control over the passions and desires that might unduly influence your actions.*

- *Your actions have consequences, and you attain ethical and moral maturity when you learn to control yourself and take **full responsibility** for all your actions.*

- *For **complex situations**, you will need to develop a reasoned capacity for ethical deliberation or the ability to weigh and sort the application of competing values.*

- *Become an ethical employer, employee and citizen.*

> **Laws control the lesser person.**
> **Right conduct controls the greater one.**
> *… Chinese proverb*

IV. **Summary**

The **good** or **evil** in **your life** is often the **result** of the **values you hold, the choices you make,** the **actions you take** and **the friends you make**. You should develop a moral code for personal behavior that is based on self-control and good core values.

- Values describe your individual personal **beliefs** and standards about what is valuable and important in life.

- Morals refer to the right or wrong of your **actions**.

- Your personal code of moral behavior, usually based on your values, should govern your conduct as regards good, bad, right, wrong, acceptable or prohibited behavior in your personal life and in your interaction with other people.

- Ethical conduct is right or wrong behavior based on a mutually **agreed upon**, sometimes written code of conduct.

- To be an accepted and respected citizen you need to embrace the values, morals and ethics of honorable people.

We can seek moral and ethical wisdom and counsel in **experience** and in the **philosophical** and **scriptural writings** of those who have gone before us. The Ten Commandments, the Golden Rule, the Silver Rule[7] and the Golden Mean are great places to start.

A personal code of high moral and ethical standards will keep you from going through life like a boat without a rudder. Lacking guidance in the storms of life, could put you way off course or sink you altogether.

Following the presentation, Mia asks if I have any idea how our souls actually progress through values, morality, ethics and virtue.

The challenge on this Earth, I think, is to educate our minds, **strengthen our wills** and **control our emotions** so that we can **withstand greater** and **greater temptation** by becoming more and **more virtuous souls**.

To do so, we must have good values, practice moral and ethical behavior, and adopt virtues while avoiding vice as much as possible.

Chapter 2 Morality and Ethics

I want to emphasize the importance of **constantly seeking to become more virtuous** because if we are not actively pursuing virtue, before we know it, we may be sliding down, ever so smoothly into sin and vice.

Most importantly, each step down into vice erodes our willpower opening the way to further decent until step by step we descend all the way into the devils of addiction and the evils of excess. Eventually, we find ourselves imprisoned in a living hell of our own making.

The ultimate purpose of life is to develop the spiritual strength to keep weakness, immorality and vice from our souls that will enable a better transformation into a closer relationship with God.

Over the courses of our lives, the process of making hundreds of moral and ethical decisions day in and day out is forging the character of our souls. It is through living these decisions and their consequences that we **purge vice** from our souls, or **add vice** to our souls, and add or lose virtue in the process.

Carter and I are working on a list of virtues and vices that we might be able to cover next month."

In the meantime, the following list of questions might help clarify acceptable and unacceptable human behaviors that may help you identify some generally accepted moral and ethical standards:

1. Do you in any way cheat, swindle or con other people?
2. Do you seek truth in all matters?
3. Are you humble? Do you think of yourself less often and of others more often?
4. Do you avoid gluttony and greed?
5. Are you selfish or self-centered?
6. Are you caring, respectful and forgiving of others?
7. Do you engage in unfair or unjust conduct?

Mayest, thou prosper in the health and blessings of a virtuous soul.

Soul's Code of Conduct

8. Do you seriously slander or insult other people or their beliefs?
9. Do you love, help, and obey your parents?
10. Do you disobey or disrespect those in authority over you?
11. Do you care for your aged parents and respect their wishes?
12. Are you teaching your children right from wrong?
13. Do you physically or mentally abuse or seriously neglect your parents or children?
14. Do you faithfully carry out the duties of your roles in life?
15. Have you killed, abused or seriously harmed anyone?
16. Have you seriously considered thoughts of suicide?
17. Do you take or sell illegal drugs?
18. Have you promoted or had an abortion?
19. Are you guilty of animal abuse and cruelty?
20. Do you commit adultery (having sex with anyone other than your spouse)?
21. Do you steal money, or the property of others?
22. If you damage people's property, do you admit it and pay for it?
23. Have you defrauded workers of their just wage?
24. Have you stolen property or, bought, or sold stolen property?
25. Have you willfully defaced or destroyed another's property?
26. Have you gambled with resources needed by your family?
27. Have you stolen your employer's time, by doing less than you are paid to do?
28. Have you inflated your expense or Per Diem Account?

Chapter 2 Morality and Ethics

29. Have you enslaved anyone?
30. Have you not repaid loans?
31. Have you pirated computer software, or bootlegged movies or have you violated other copyright laws?
32. Have you bribed anyone, or accepted a bribe?
33. Are you guilty of excessive waste or expense?
34. Have you blackmailed anyone?
35. Have you committed forgery?
36. Are you guilty of fraud or embezzlement?
37. Have you evaded or cheated on your tax payments?
38. Are you guilty of price fixing or collusion?
39. Do you tell lies about other people's behavior?
40. Do you tell any other serious or premeditated lies?
41. Do you gossip about other people's faults?
42. Have you violated the confidence of someone without reason?
43. Do you lust after someone else's husband or wife?
44. Do you willfully lust after anyone other than your spouse?
45. Do you seriously seek after someone else's possessions?
46. Have you committed crimes by violating criminal or civil laws?

The appendix to this book contains a good discussion of universal human moral standards that should help those interested in intentionally improving the quality of their souls.

**It's not so hard to make decisions
once you know what your values are.**
...Roy Disney

Moral Compass

<u>**A well-developed conscience is a moral compass for all time.**</u>

**The desire of power in excess caused the angels to fall;
the desire of knowledge in excess caused man to fall, but in goodness there
is no excess, neither can angel or man come in danger by it.**
... Sir Francis Bacon Essay on Goodness XIII

Some research indicates that people judge what is morally right or wrong based on five basic moral dimensions:[8]

1. **Care** - kindness and caring about others

2. **Fairness** - fair and just treatment of people

3. **Loyalty** - to groups like family, team or nation

4. **Respect for Legitimate Authority** - traditions and government

5. **Spiritual Sanctity** - actions believed to be inherently right or wrong on a sacred and holy basis.

Not everyone considers all five of these criteria. For example, the research suggests that politically liberal people usually consider only the first two while political conservatives tend to take into account all five. In their moral deliberations, people also are likely to give differing weight to the various dimensions.

Chapter 2 Morality and Ethics

We should all seek to be in control of our thoughts and desires and masters of our wills while living with a quiet unobtrusive dignity and consideration for others.

Remember the real danger of the slippery slope is that minor transgressions can snowball into cataclysmic ones. For example, according to the Josephson Institute, kids who cheat on high school exams are three times more likely to become dishonest adults.[5]

Thank you for sitting in on our seminar on morality and ethics. I hope it was worth your time.

Meanwhile, the new Socialist U.S. economy is getting worse with much higher taxes, and escalating prices of many goods and services. In addition, growing shortages of food and medicine are beginning to affect us here at the base camp.

History shows that the gravest threat to a free people's liberty is their own government, as creeping socialism and overspending lead to totalitarian dictatorship.

---

[1] Professor Clancy Martin, *Moral Decision Making*, The Teaching Company, Chantilly VA. 2008 course guidebook p.5. For Bishop Joseph Butler see p.104

[2] Ibid p.87

[3] Caroline Myss, *Anatomy of the Spirit*, Crown Publishers p.81

[4] Professor Steven Erickson, *Philosophy as a Guide to Living*, The Teaching Company, Chantilly VA Course Guidebook p.115

[5] Josephson Institute josephsoninstitute.org/policing/overview/faq.html

[6] http://josephsoninstitute.org

[7] The **Silver Rule**, "Do not do unto others what you would not have them do unto you," is a standard of behavior found in the writings of, amongst others, Hillel the Elder (Talmud, *Shabbat* 31a). http://www.ask.com/wiki/Silver_Rule?qsrc=3044&lang=en

[8] Professor Mark Leary, *Why You Are Who You Are*, The Teaching Company, Chantilly VA 2018 Course 1648 Guidebook p.79

Chapter 3

Virtue and Vice

While Carter is entering inventory data into a computer, the front door bell rings. He opens the door and is surprised to find the most beautiful young woman he has ever seen. He quickly invites her in and asks if she would like a cup of coffee.

Smiling, she replies, "I could really use one just now, thank you."

Minutes later, they are enjoying a hot cup of java together. Carter is captivated; her voice is velvety and low for a woman's and very appealing. She has scintillating dark hair and dreamboat eyes with dark attractive eyebrows and long eyelashes.

So enchanted is Carter, that he cannot keep his mind on what she is saying. Embarrassed, he has to ask her to repeat herself several times.

Finally, he is able to pay attention long enough to find out that she is a medical student interested in alternative medicine who would like to meet Dr. Moses. And, if possible, she would like to spend some time learning about alternative medicine from him.

She says she wants to learn all she can from him since he has a growing reputation as one of the foremost practitioners of alternative medicine in the world. Her father is a doctor, and she says she can pay for her instruction.

To overcome fear, be overwhelmingly grateful
...Sir John Templeton

"By the way, my name is Claire," says she extending her hand. Carter shook her hand and feels an electric current pulsate through his arm, causing him to forget momentarily to let go of her hand.

"Boy, she must think I am a dunce," he thinks, even as he hears her ask his name for the second time.

"Oh, ah it's Carter," he says. "It's Carter."

"Well, Carter is the doctor here today?" she asks.

"No," he says, "Doc left this morning on an overnight trip, but I expect him back tomorrow afternoon."

"In that case," says she, "I will need a motel room for the night. Is there a motel nearby that you can recommend?"

"Oh yes, as a matter of fact there is," says Carter. "We have guest quarters right here on the property, for we occasionally receive visitors."

"Oh, I couldn't take a room that might be needed," says Claire.

"But we have two, both are empty, and there are no visitors scheduled for a while," says Carter with conviction.

"Well, okay," she says, "if you're sure it will be alright and just for one night."

"Super," beams Carter, "may I help you bring in some things?"

"If it's not too much trouble, it would be appreciated," responds Claire. "I am on my way home from my first year of medical school at UVa, so the car is packed. When I realized I was passing nearby, I decided to take a chance on at least meeting the Enlightened Physician."

"If there be no virtue among us, no form of government can render us secure. To suppose that any form of government will secure liberty or happiness without virtue in the people is an illusion."
…. *James Madison 4th President of the United States and "Father of the Constitution"*

"Doc is a great guy," says Carter. "He is making such a difference in the lives of so many people, yet he remains humble and easy to be with. We all live here in this complex of buildings that we call the base camp, so we really get to know one another on a personal basis."

"How many people work here with you and the doctor?" she inquires.

"We have five others including my best friend Warden, who handles appointments, applications for Doc's help, scheduling and out of town travel arrangements.

"Then there are two medical surgical interns: Mia and Ashley who help Doc and keep up with the medical records. We also have a first class cook named Laura who buys and prepares all the food and a part time handyman and computer whiz named Bill."

"What is your role?" asks Claire.

"Well, I raise funds; handle the finance and accounting, payroll, taxes, purchasing and public relations as well as legal issues. I also keep track of the controlled substances. I established a non-profit foundation for Doc and donated my buildings and this property to it.

"Therefore, I try to make sure the property is well maintained though Bill does much of the work," adds Carter. "We have a first class, two-way satellite and fiber optic video communications network that allows Doc to help people all over the world, and Bill and I take care of the network."

"It sounds like you have your hands full," she says.

"Not really, we are all on a mission here, and the work just doesn't seem like work. We are like-minded people dedicated to a cause much bigger than ourselves."

"What about you, Claire? What do you like to do when you are not in medical school studying?"

> **"Remember that the happiest people are not those getting more, but those giving more."**
> *...H. Jackson Brown Jr.*

Chapter 3 Virtue and Vice

"Now don't laugh," she remarks, "but I am interested in spiritual things. I almost went into the ministry, but decided on medicine instead."

Carter about fell out of his chair. As if her awesome good looks and charm aren't enough, they even share the same interests.

"Wow, that's neat," he says.

They stay up late talking and sharing information. She is amazed at his background, especially the four years as an Ascetic.

By midnight, he trusts her enough to share the Manual of the Soul with her, and they each retire for the night. The next morning early, she reads the manual with intense interest and enthusiasm. She finds herself looking forward to seeing Carter again, thinking, "He's not as dumb as he first seemed."

At nine o'clock, Carter calls the room and invites Claire to breakfast, which is Eggs Benedict. Over the meal, they talk about many things and afterward, Carter brings her up to date on the monthly seminars they've been doing. He mentions that this weekend they will be doing one on virtue and vice.

"Oh," she says, "I would love to hear that; so many of my friends are struggling with that battle, and there isn't much known about it, at least not among my generation. Everyone is into social media and video entertainment, so most people don't read anything they don't have to, which generally leaves out moral philosophy."

"Why not stay for the weekend?" intones Carter earnestly. "It's Thursday already, and it would be so cool if you could stay and participate."

"Well, let's see what the doctor says," she responds discreetly.

> **Pride, as in smugness or over-inflated self-importance leads to every other vice. It is the complete anti-God state of mind.**
> ...Professor C.S. Lewis

They soon found out, as Doc and the others arrive on schedule. Doc is impressed with Claire's quick mind and selfless attitude, and he invites her to stay for the weekend.

Claire calls her parents to let them know where she is, and that she will be home a few days later than originally planned. Warden returns Friday afternoon and is soon enchanted by Claire as well.

Friday evening after dinner, Carter begins the following presentation on Virtue and vice:

Handbook of the Soul

Virtue and Vice

I. Preview

Virtues are firm habits of good conduct, and Vices are firm habits of bad conduct.

- We can acquire virtue by replacing selfish thoughts and bad habits with **virtuous thoughts and good habits.**

> "A man is happy, wise and great in the measure that he controls himself; he is wretched, foolish and mean in the measure that he allows his animal nature to dominate his thoughts and actions."
> *…Philosopher James Allen*

- We must make a habit of virtuous thinking because the thoughts that inhabit our minds establish the **deep-seated values of our souls that help determine our conduct.**

- The deep-seated values and habits of our soul establish our **character** affecting the **course** of our human and subsequent lives.

II. Introduction

Previously when we discussed values, morality and ethics, we noted the following:

1. *Values are the principles and activities you care about most that form your guiding beliefs and convictions.*

2. *Morals (right and wrong behavior), refer to your standards of personal and social behavior that are usually based on your values.*

3. *Ethics, while similar, usually refer to a somewhat more formal, generally **agreed upon** code of behavior.*

III. Virtue and Vice Defined

*Virtues are **established habits** that have become character traits of a particular good behavior such as generosity or honesty. Human character traits reside in the soul.*

*Vices, on the other hand, are **established habits** or character traits of a particular bad behavior such as cheating or being critical of others, and they also reside in the soul. Key words being **established habits**.*

- *All the knowledge in the world about virtue will not a virtue make.*

- *The development of virtue requires the action of cultivation, of growing the virtue by your repeated and consistent choice of a particular honorable action.*

"Our greatness is not so much in being able to remake the world,
as in being able to remake ourselves."
... *Spiritual leader Mahatma Gandhi*

- It has been said that **habit** is a cable, and you weave a thread of it every day, until at last you cannot break it.

IV. Developing Virtue

Virtue is developed by forming ingrained **habits** of good, moral and ethical behavior. With free will, you are free to choose to think and behave in either of the following ways:

- Self-strengthening, positive and morally correct modes of behavior that build virtue into the eternal character of your soul
- Selfish, negative and regressive ways that build vice to weaken and erode the eternal character of your soul

Progress occurs if you develop the spiritual strength and wisdom to recognize and choose, more frequently and consistently, the moral, positive operating modes of life and to reject more often the negative and selfish ones.

Virtue is an achievement of character to be accomplished through proper training and practiced within a social order initially grounded in the family. All good social interaction is **grounded in virtue** that reflects excellence in a social context.

Repeated Right Choices - Virtues are attained by the process of moral development that comes with the sustained repetition of a particular morally good and right decision each time you are faced with the same type of moral choice. Once it becomes such a habit, for instance, that you make the decision not to lie, without giving it a second thought, then you have established a virtue of telling the truth.

Sickness of the Soul - A vice, on the other hand, can be understood as a sickness of the soul due to poor self-control. Actions born of vice weaken and decay the spiritual power of the soul.

Looking back on his life, Jack Par said
it seemed like living was just one lifelong obstacle course
with myself being the main obstacle.

Chapter 3 Virtue and Vice

Vice is the habit of repeatedly making the same destructive, immoral, unethical or otherwise poor choice to misbehave in the same way, such as lying whenever it is convenient to do so.

Self-control - *Is the first requirement for the development of virtue.*

- *Self-control is the power of gathering, focusing and compelling mental energy into self-determined, virtuous thought that leads to beneficial activity. She who controls her thinking controls her life.*

- *Allowing thinking to wander and follow the line of least resistance leads it to the tempting channels of vice.*

- *The best way to deal with temptation is to avoid it altogether. It is much easier to avoid the **door** leading to a tempting vice than it is to overcome a close encounter with the vice or sin itself.*

- *We must keep away from the doors that lead to the temptations, for instance those fighting prostitution should stay out of the places where prostitutes are located. Those fighting gluttony should avoid the kitchen door, and those fighting alcoholism should stay out of bars, pubs and liquor stores. Make your stand just out of temptations reach, where the battle is more easily won.*

Fear and Anxiety - *Fear and anxiety are vices that condition many people's lives to heightened levels of confusion and hatred. Choices we make contain the **energy** of either **faith** or **fear**, and **each has the power to affect our thinking and our actions**.*

- *Fear reduces our ability to relate with confidence to the external world.*

- *The voice of fear hypnotizes us, and we are unable to think or act with clarity.*

- *We are contaminated with fears that short-circuit creative energy and ideas.*

- *Unfortunately, the vices of fear and anxiety usually go unrecognized by their owners.*

The antidote to all vice is virtue, which leads to lives that are much more peaceful, meaningful and beneficial.

Soul's Code of Conduct

SELF-CONTROL

DOOR TO HEAVEN

Self-control is the door to heaven.
...Renowned Philosopher James Allen

<u>Self-control</u> - the transformation of your character and your soul is not instantaneous nor is it always a pleasant and painless process.

- *God and nature demand effort and patience as the price of growth.*

- *However, if we could only understand how closely and inseparably self–control and happiness are linked, there would be an end to much unhappiness in this life.*

We must learn that we cannot command things, but we can command ourselves; we should not try to coerce the wills of others, but we can be the master our own willpower.

<u>Freedom and Obligation</u> - Unlike animals that must rely on inborn instinct, you have the freedom and the obligation to choose your own patterns of right or wrong (moral) behavior.

It can take hard, challenging spiritual work, perseverance and dedication to develop virtuous habits. You will have to use will power, courage and self-control to develop habits of virtue instead of vice.

<u>Easier Habits of Vice</u> - If you are not very careful, it will be much easier to fall into the bad habits of vice without necessarily making a conscious choice to do so. For instance, you could develop a bad and unethical habit of not paying your bills because you unintentionally spend more money than you earn.

- However, your actions have consequences even if they are unintentional actions.

- It is a great deal easier to develop the right habits in the first place than to have to undo bad habits later on.

- We have a moral duty to establish a virtuous mindset as part of the formation of a well-ordered soul.

Virtue does not just happen to us. It is a mindset that we must develop. Vice, on the other hand, can seem just to happen, and it will unless you are actively working against it.

**Treat people as if they were what they ought to be,
and you contribute to their becoming the best they can be.**
…Writer and Statesman Johann Wolfgang von Goethe

Unethical vice - Virtue and vice include, but also extend beyond, your ethical and moral habits.

- For example, a bad habit of overeating is a vice of gluttony but not an unethical vice because it doesn't involve taking unfair advantage of other people.
- A bad habit of lying to people is an unethical vice.
- The bad habit of sexual promiscuity is an immoral vice involving lust and immodesty.

Virtue is said to be its own reward because learning to live a life of virtue will have a positive, transformational effect on your soul.

Animal Like - Wickedness and vice demean the weak, self-indulgent person and diminish his or her soul back toward the animal like phase of human existence.

Restraint or Temperance - is the virtue that ensures that we desire what faith and reason recognize as good, and that we reject that which faith and reason recognize as bad. The virtue of **courage** can ensure that we overcome the challenges and obstacles to our attainment of what faith and reason recognize as good.

Clay in the Hands - Without strong virtues such as Wisdom, Courage and Moderation to guide them, people are just clay in the hands of circumstance that will mold them into weak and wavering things it can blow about as leaves in the wind.[1] So, develop the gravitas to anchor your soul with the weight of virtue and good character!

Laura asks Carter if it was not possible to live a life of neither virtue nor vice. Carter said, "We are very likely to fall into vice unless we are trying hard to pursue virtue."

The consensus was that even if a neutral life were possible, it might not help much with the transformation of one's soul toward a closer relationship with God.

> "It's in the moments of your decisions that your destiny is shaped."
> ...Author Anthony Robbins

V. Categories of Virtue & Vice

(See glossary in book 1 for definitions of the virtues and vices noted below)

A. <u>Eight Virtues of Life</u> - *The following five classical virtues plus three theological virtues, taken together, could be called the Eight Virtues of Life since they encompass the keys to a life well lived.*

Five Classical Virtues:

Wisdom, Courage, Moderation, Justice and Prudence

Three Theological virtues:

Faith, Hope and Love

B. <u>Seven Deadly Sins</u> – *The following so called "Seven Deadly Sins" are the worst human tendencies or vices at the root of our being that if not overcome will deform our souls and condemn us to the animal stage of existence:*

1. Selfishness and Pride
2. Envy
3. Anger
4. Laziness
5. Greed
6. Gluttony
7. Lust

The ancient Greek philosopher Plato observed that in a well-ordered human soul, reason assisted by emotional control and restraint rule the lower appetites of gluttony, lust and drunkenness.

Plato taught that if we discipline the passions, reign in our feelings and look out for the common good, virtue would develop leading to genuine happiness, good feelings and community.

> "The interior joy we feel when we have done a good deed is the nourishment the soul requires."
> *...Philosopher and Physician Albert Schweitzer*

Habits of Excellence - Plato's most famous student Aristotle observed that moral excellence comes about as a result of habits of excellence, noting that the way we become just is by regularly doing just things.

The way to become moderate is by maintaining a moderate disposition and doing things in a moderate way, and the way to develop the virtue of courage is by repeatedly doing morally and ethically courageous things.[2]

Ethical Moral Confusion - Many unethical and immoral decisions, said Carter, result not from confusion, but from a lack of willpower or a weak character. We do something even though we know it is wrong. We just want some things more than we want to do what is right.[3]

Four Moral Tests - In case of confusion, however, the **following four moral tests** can be used to help clarify a proper and virtuous choice:

1. The Moral Hazard Test – Are you considering taking risks because any negative consequences of your action will fall only on others?

2. The Publicity Test – What would you do if you knew your conduct was to be reported to the public?

3. The "If Everyone Did It" Test - According to the philosopher Immanuel Kant, a test to apply to moral and ethical decisions is to ask if what you are considering doing would be a good thing if everyone did it.

4. The Parent Test - Another good moral and ethical check is the Parent Test.

- If your child did what you're thinking of doing, would you be proud or disappointed?

- If your children knew what you were going to do, would they be disappointed in you?

- If your child was in the same situation and asked your advice, what would you say?

Father of Philosophy, Socrates said wisdom is realizing humbly how little you know, not proudly thinking you know much more than you do.

- If your mother were looking over your shoulder, what would you do?

<u>Exertion of Spirit and Mind</u> - *The meaning of life is to be found in the opportunity it provides for us to train ourselves to establish habits of virtue in as many specific traits of our character as possible. It can become second nature to make good, fair and prudent choices about right and wrong (moral) behavior.*

Developing habits of virtue often requires maximum exertion of spirit and mind; however, it is worth the effort because it ultimately determines who we become.

By imagining what an ideal character of virtue might be, we can set our lives on a course toward that ideal.

- Even though we may come up short of the ideal, we will be moving in the right direction.
- The closer we can strive to the ideal character of highest virtue, the more meaningful our lives will be. Use the checklist on subsequent pages to rate yourself on each of the character traits of virtue and vice.

Carter says it's time for another break.

While on the break, Warden says to Carter, "I am struggling every day trying to fit people into Doc's crowded schedule that's now six months out. Many are dying before I can get them on the schedule, while others on the schedule die before Doc gets to them."

"I have begun to doubt myself and my worthiness to keep making these life and death decisions that are affecting so many people."

"However," Warden added, "these seminars are helping to reassure me that it's not my unworthiness or poor decision making that's contributing to the growing number of deaths."

**Think no vice so small that you may commit it, and
no virtue so small that you may overlook it.**
...*Chinese Philosopher Confucius*

"It's more like vices of fear and doubt that I must overcome in my own life, in order to keep helping Doc who hasn't had a real break in years."

They decide the workload is a serious problem and something has to be done about it soon.

Getting back to the seminar, Carter presents a chart of Virtues and Vices.

VI. Chart of Thirty-Eight Virtues and Vices of Life

*Presented on pages below is an inventory of **Thirty-Eight** common **Virtues and Vices** that you can use to evaluate the current state of your own character. These are a representative but not exclusive list of virtues and vices presented in the following three categories:*

- A. ***Personal Virtues** and **Vices*** *- The first 16 of the 38 are personal virtues and vices of an internal nature having to do with your personal disposition. This involves thinking and self-control of the more personal characteristics of your soul.*

- B. ***Interpersonal Virtues** and **Vices*** *– The next thirteen are interpersonal virtues and vices that involve our treatment or mistreatment of other people.*

- C. ***Personal / Interpersonal Virtues** and **Vices*** *- Finally, the last nine might fit both categories, so they are considered Personal / Interpersonal Virtues and Vices.*

*In many cases, you may find that you have neither the fully trained habits of virtue nor the settled bad habits of vice. In such cases, you may be somewhere in between, **still struggling to make the more virtuous choices each day.***

Evaluating Your Character *- You can evaluate the current state of your character by rating each of your character traits as a virtue, a vice or an uncertainty.*

>It is easier to build strong children than
>it is to repair broken adults.
>*...Educator Frederick Douglas*

Chapter 3 Virtue and Vice

*Rate each of the following 38-character traits **on a percentage** of the time you think you act with virtue or vice.*

At the top of the chart, the first trait "Productive" (hard working) is used as an example and is shown on a percentage of time scale.

- *If **most** of the time you are productive when you should be, then you might estimate that you have the virtue of productivity or working hard maybe 70% of the time.*

- *Maybe you are lazy about 10% of the time when you should be doing something useful (a vice of 10%).*

- *Maybe you are uncertain about what you do the rest of the time when you should be doing something productive (20% uncertain).*

The sum of virtue, uncertainty and vice must total 100% for each character trait as 70%, 20% and 10% add up to 100% in the example.

Any trait rated as virtuous over 90% of the time could be considered a **character virtue**, but be aware of the human tendency to overrate ourselves.

The challenge for every single human being is to **master** the **virtues** and to **purge the vices**. For a discussion of universal moral standards, please refer to the appendix.

1987 Vatican 20 Lire "Forbidden Fruit" coin

"Good Character is more to be praised than outstanding talent. Most talents are to some extent a gift. Good character, by contrast, is not given to us. We have to build it piece by piece
– by thought, choice, courage and determination."
...Theologian John Luther

Virtues and Vices of the Human Soul

On the next three pages are many of the virtues and vices that come into play in the lives of most human beings.

A. Personal Virtues and Vices

Virtue		Vice	Virtue	Uncertainty	Vice
1. Productive	vs.	Lazy	70%	20%	10%
2. Joyful	vs.	Depressed	------	------	------
3. Hopeful	vs.	Despairing	------	------	------
4. Faith filled	vs.	Fearful/Anxious	------	------	------
5. Humble	vs.	Arrogant	------	------	------
6. Humorous	vs.	Humorless	------	------	------
7. Optimistic	vs.	Pessimistic	------	------	------
8. Patient	vs.	Impatient	------	------	------
9. Disciplined	vs.	Un-disciplined	------	------	------
10. Dutiful	vs.	Irresponsible	------	------	------
11. Moderate	vs.	Excessive	------	------	------
12. Prudent	vs.	Reckless	------	------	------
13. Restrained	vs.	Gluttonous	------	------	------
14. Sober	vs.	Drunken	------	------	------
15. Chaste	vs.	Promiscuous	------	------	------
16. Wise	vs.	Foolish	------	------	------

According to Philosopher James Allen, the nobler moral qualities of virtue are man's liberators; it is well that he should use them to overcome and stamp out the vices such as sexual immorality, thievery, greed, drunkenness, lying, cheating, etc. that hold his soul in bondage to weakness, moral squalor and degradation."

B. Interpersonal Virtues and Vices

Virtues		Vices	Virtue	Uncertainty	Vice
17. Unselfish	vs.	Selfish	------	------	------
18. Forgiving	vs.	Unforgiving	------	------	------
19. Sympathetic	vs.	Indifferent	------	------	------
20. Loving	vs.	Hateful	------	------	------
21. Generous	vs.	Stingy / Greedy	------	------	------
22. Kind	vs.	Cruel	------	------	------
23. Honest	vs.	Deceitful	------	------	------
24. Respectful	vs.	Disrespectful	------	------	------
25. Agreeable	vs.	Disagreeable	------	------	------
26. Encouraging	vs.	Critical/judging	------	------	------
27. Concise	vs.	Talkative	------	------	------
28. Just	vs.	Unjust	------	------	------
29. Contented	vs.	Envious	------	------	------

VII. Identifying Character Weaknesses

These three checklists can be used to self-identify your strengths (virtues) weaknesses (vices) and the uncertain, unresolved areas of your character that are currently neither virtue nor vice, but will eventually become one or the other.

- The extent to which you frequently operate in any of the vices of life can help you determine which aspects of your character may be weak and in need of improvement.

- A good, objective evaluation of your weaknesses or vices can provide a clear agenda for conscious improvement in your character.

C. **Personal / Interpersonal Virtues and Vices**

Virtues	Vices	Virtue	Uncertainty	Vice
30. Harmonious vs.	Ill-tempered	------	------	------
31. Calm vs.	Angry	------	------	------
32. Courageous vs.	Cowardly	------	------	------
33. Creative vs.	Destructive	------	------	------
34. Honorable vs.	Dishonorable	------	------	------
35. Modest vs.	Lustful / Wanton	------	------	------
36. Thankful vs.	Ungrateful	------	------	------
37. Righteous vs.	Evil	------	------	------
38. Positive vs.	Negative	------	------	------

Unfortunately, it may be difficult for you to recognize some of your own weaknesses, so you should work hard to develop the personal courage and integrity to evaluate yourself honestly.

You must withdraw your critical fault-finding capacity from its application to the opinions and conduct of others and apply it with equal rigor to yourself. Ask a friend or relative who knows you well to help but don't hold their honesty against them!

Generosity *is an important virtue to start with because the act of giving enables us to lessen our attachment to things and to ourselves. It helps us act out an understanding that we are not the center of the universe.*

- *Positivity vs negativity refers to our **mental attitude** because much of our **unhappiness** is **due** to our own mental **attitudes**.*
- *Therefore, we can lead better lives by **changing our attitudes** instead of trying to change the world and the attitudes of the other people in it.*
- *As one ancient sage put it: if it hurts to walk on the hard and rocky earth, you can either try to cover in leather all the world or you can cover in leather your own two feet.*

- *Finally, the **virtue of patience** is of great importance because it is the antidote to anger. It is also an essential virtue for those who are seriously committed to moral cultivation because self-transformation is a long and arduous path that often demands patience.*

*In addition, if we want to help others overcome their irrational anger; we cannot do so by adding our own anger on top of theirs. We at all times should **build one another up** with **inspiration** and **encouragement***

Warden's comments about the workload and the fact that Doc has been working without time off for years is a concern to all. Carter suggests that they start training up other people to take some of the load from Doc. What complicates matters was that Doc has been enlightened in ways that give him intuitive powers that might not be transferable.

Nevertheless, if someone works closely under Doc's supervision, and if Doc tries to teach him or her, what he can explain, then surely, such a person might end up carrying part of the load. If things work out well, Doc might even get a few weeks of vacation each year.

Doc says he would prefer someone with basic medical training, but not so much that he or she is no longer open to alternative medicine. Doc asks the team to think about it and typically goes back to work.

Getting back to the seminar, Carter lists the following insights on virtue inspired by British philosopher James Allen's excellent book "The Life Triumphant" about faithful and courageous living through self-control.[4]

1. Self-control with quiet dignity and consideration for others is the mark of a mature human being. Cultivate and foster virtues; honor others and respect yourself.

"Perfection is not attainable,
but if we chase perfection, we can catch excellence."
...Legendary Football Coach Vince Lombardi

2. Each human being has a limited amount of energy that can be used or misused, conserved and concentrated or dissipated and dispersed. It is a universal law that energy used in one direction is not available for use in other directions.

3. Vice must be rejected if virtue is to be attained. The energy wasted in a fit of bad temper reduces the power in the person's store of virtue just as the time and energy wasted in idleness is not available for work. Some people squander themselves in excesses---in bad tempers, hatreds, gluttonous, unworthy and illicit pleasures--- and then they blame life for their poor circumstances.

4. Virtuous people put a check upon themselves and they set a watch upon their passions and emotions. In this way, they gain full possession of their souls and little by little achieve a steady calmness of spirit and fullness of life.

5. Only they that can conquer themselves, who strive, day by day, after more self-control, and greater tranquility of mind can attain great virtue. Self-control is gained by constant practice. We must surmount our weaknesses by daily effort. We must know ourselves and learn how to purge weakness and vice from within us.

6. Slowly and arduously, your **soul** can be **strengthened** by living properly through the ups and downs of life's long process of **purification**. Gradually power, serenity and calm descend upon the souls that grow in virtue. Serenity born of great spiritual strength is the true sign of a virtuous and enlightened soul.

7. There are many unknowing **hypocrites** that thoughtlessly fall victim to **insincerity**, which undermines happiness and weakens the moral fabric of their characters.

8. Mankind's conquest of land provides earthly dwellings, but the **conquest of self** creates a mansion for **eternity**.

9. The vice of **fear** can scare us into relying on material things rather than on spiritual things for our security. The antidote, of course, is the virtue of **faith**.

VIII. Two Step Process for Developing Virtue

Once your vices are identified, the process of improvement can begin. Conscious character improvement is a two-step process.

- **First**, you must **think often** enough about the character trait or vice you wish to improve to cause a twinge of your conscience or a mental alert to occur whenever a relevant decision or choice arises involving the vice you are trying to eliminate.

- This first step may take a period of several weeks depending on how often each day you think about your goal.

- The **second step** is to **change behavior** as a result of the mental alerts or twinges of conscience. For example, if selfishness was the vice a woman wanted to change, she should start thinking, off and on for weeks, about the need to be less selfish.

- After thinking about her goal for a while, she should start getting vague mental suggestions from her conscience, perhaps while shopping, that she should consider buying less clothing for herself and something instead for others such as family members or friends.

<u>**Well Timed Messages**</u> - She might ignore or overlook the suggestions at first, but if she keeps thinking about the need to be less selfish, the well-timed messages from her conscience will become more frequent and less subtle. They will likely continue until she starts making less selfish decisions that change her behavior.

- If, over time, she continues to make progress until she has developed permanently less selfish habits, the result will be a conscious improvement in her eternal character.

- If no progress is made and her behavior is never changed, her conscience will eventually become insensitive to it.

"**If you want your dream to come true, you must wake up.**"
…Anonymous

Another example might involve a man who wants to control his temper.

If he thinks frequently about the goal of controlling his temper, he will soon start to get a quick mental caution message just before he explodes into an angry outburst.

- *At first, he might not be able to catch himself in time, but he will eventually do so if he keeps trying.*
- *With concerted effort and continued thinking about his goal, his behavior can begin to change.*
- *His bad habit will eventually change and ultimately through this process he will have eliminated a serious vice and improved his character.*

Making permanent changes in some deeply ingrained negative character traits (vices) may be difficult, and it may require a great deal of patience and determination.

IX. Quality of the Person You Are Becoming

No one can be expected to become perfect, but the more difficult the circumstances under which you can think, feel and act in a positive, virtuous and graceful manner, the more progress you make in the development of your soul.

Much of your human challenge, purpose and mission is to learn to operate, as much as possible, in the graceful, virtuous, positive modes of life.

- *Spiritual strength comes from overcoming the negative aspects of life with grace, faith and the constant application of positive and virtuous life principles.*
- *It's under the challenging stress of very difficult circumstances, great temptation, other negative people or poor personal health, that we can make great progress.*

Trying situations sometimes last for extended periods and require increasingly greater amounts of spiritual will and stamina.

Faith, prayer, physical exercise and a focus on the needs of other people are examples of proven methods to sustain a positive spiritual attitude in the face of extended personal adversity.

- Each moral decision you make involving right or wrong, no matter how small, is **helping shape the quality of the person you are becoming**.

- For example, suppose you have a choice between only two remaining slices of pizza, one cheese, (which you prefer) and the other pepperoni.

- You know that one of the other people present cannot eat the pepperoni, so which do you take?

Before you decide, ask yourself who you are and what type person you want to be, gracious or selfish, and choose accordingly.

The vice and failures of character that cause and result from poor choices are not condemnations to continual failure. They are just misuses of your energy that will cause more difficulty in life.

Negative thoughts, words and wrong decisions shape your character a bit in the wrong direction, which means it will require that many more positive thoughts, words and favorable choices to reshape your character back in the right direction.

- Do you like yourself?
- If not, what don't you like about yourself, and why?
- Are you actively working to change the things you don't like?

X. Scriptural Family Virtues

The following mostly domestic admonitions are examples of virtuous direction found in various scriptures:

1. Husbands love your wives as yourself, live with her in a kind way, and honor her in all ways as your wife.

"Restraint stops negative feelings, and virtue promotes positive feelings."
...The 14th Dali Lama

2. *Wives be subject to your husbands; respect them in all ways, honor their wishes, and be cheerful and supportive of them.*

3. *Children, obey your parents and honor your father and mother.*

4. *Fathers bring up your children in the discipline and instruction of the Almighty.*

5. *Employees obey your employers with a sincere heart, and be well pleasing, not argumentative, not pilfering but performing your work in good faith and with your best effort.*

6. *Adult men are to be sober-minded, dignified, self-controlled, sound in faith, in love and in steadfastness.*

7. *Adult women likewise are to be reverent in behavior, not slanderers or slaves to wine. They are to teach what is good and so train the young women to be kind and to love their future husbands. Children are to be taught self-control.*

8. *Younger men and women are to be self-controlled with integrity, dignity, and speech that cannot be condemned.*

9. *Finally let all humankind be righteous, have compassion, sympathy and brotherly love one for another, a tender heart and a humble mind. Do not repay evil for evil or reviling for reviling, but on the contrary, bless those who oppose you, that you may be blessed also.*

XI. Summary

Carter summarized by observing that we are not necessarily born or raised with great morality and virtue.

- We can acquire high virtue and strong morality at any age by replacing selfish thoughts and bad habits with good thoughts and virtuous habits.

- It takes **courage** and **persistence**, as well as self-control and the application of spiritual discipline to **master** the **Thirty-Eight Virtues of the Human Soul**.

"Life isn't about finding yourself. Life is about making yourself."
---Author George Bernard Shaw

- *Some people believe that virtue forms the fabric of heaven and the true spiritual realm of the soul, and that we must become like that again in order to return to it.[5]*

- *Developing habits of virtue in your ethical and moral behavior will lead to significant and admirable character improvement that will enable a greater spiritual transformation within your soul during your earthly experience.*

- *Developing habits of virtue often requires maximum exertion of spirit and mind, but it will ultimately determine who each of us, in truth, can say we are!*

A life well lived honors God and inspires others, and it benefits the one who lives it. A gracious and virtuous character is a treasure for all time that will enable you truly to enjoy life and a much more enlightened relationship with the Divine.

Positive Mental Attitude - Good character begins with a positive mental attitude and the discipline to **control the thought process deep in your soul.** This, so that you have a loving, unselfish, positive outlook on life instead of a fearful, anxious, selfish or negative outlook.

Improving the character of your soul takes time, prayer and perseverance for it is truly the project of a lifetime! A completely virtuous soul is an ideal toward which we can all aspire and strive to approximate. Thanks to you all for participating in this Seminar!

A record of the seminar has been sent to the Colonel for his input and inclusion in the journal. He notes that you can almost feel the evolution of your soul taking place during those very brief moments while you consider each of the moral and ethical choices you make.

Everyone on the staff is there because they are attracted to the mission, but also because they know Doc is spiritually gifted. Like Carter and Warden, they too are interested in matters of the spirit and soul. The seminars help amplify and focus the discussions.

> "He, who wants little, always has enough."
> ...Johann Georg Ritter von Zimmermann

Claire has a great time with the team on the weekend. On the drive home to Wilmington, she spends a lot of time thinking about what she has seen in Carter's and Warden's journal and what was presented in the seminar on virtue and vice.

Claire realizes that she has a real thirst for knowledge about such things, and that there is very little said about spiritual matters in the largely secular society of the day.

Claire is thrilled to meet Doctor Moses because she recognizes in the man a physician of great talent and insight. She tells her parents all about it and is pleased to get a phone call from Carter making sure she got home all right.

During high school and college, Claire had remained focused on her studies with little time for male companionship and dating. She found men to be largely interested in only one thing, and it was not medicine, moral philosophy or anything else that mattered to her. However, Carter may be different; he is clearly focused on the things that matter in life.

Our now Socialist U.S. economy continues to worsen with shortages of everything from food to toilet paper. The Socialist politicians try giving everyone a plentiful allowance of free money, which works briefly until it causes hyper-inflation that eventually increases prices over a thousand percent. Gasoline is now over $100 a gallon, a loaf of bread is over $300 and there have been food riots in the streets.

We are now raising much of our own food in a garden, and everyone in the country is on a forced diet due to the food shortages. In trying to micro manage everyone's life and businesses; the Socialist administration has created three new problems for every one they tried to solve. Social justice for all is becoming hunger and poverty for all.

They have eliminated the natural and efficient incentives of Free Market Capitalism with its checks and balances that kept supply and demand more or less in balance through the constant unrestricted movement of prices.

"Every problem is a character–building opportunity, and the more difficult it is, the greater the potential for building spiritual muscle and fiber."
...Pastor Rick Warren in The Purpose Driven Life

They froze the free-market pricing mechanism that would head off most shortages and surpluses automatically. They killed **critical incentives** like the profit motive to motivate people to take the risks of starting and running efficient businesses. Last but not least, they destroyed the competition that helped keep prices low and then strangled the economy with a flood of senseless and costly regulations that closed more businesses and forced prices even higher.

Instead of efficient market Capitalism, they are now trying to control an economy of 350 million people with Socialism and government edicts that have created shortages, hyperinflation, a massive costly and inefficient government bureaucracy and high taxes to pay for it.

The high taxes and regulations have driven out so many businesses that there are shortages of almost everything. So now, the government is using profit controls that will further remove the incentive to produce, leading to ever more shortages.

In short, they have replaced the most productive, prosperity producing Capitalist economy in the world with a frustrating, poverty producing Socialist nightmare. All in the name of "Social Justice" and economic equity. At this rate we are all going to be equal for sure, equally poor and hungry that is. Except of course for the government officials who have given themselves special food, clothing, transportation and housing allowances conveniently adjusted to inflation. So, they are actually benefitting from everyone else's misery.

> **Liberty is linked to wisdom, so when a free man is unwise or ignores what he should know, unhealthy desires start taking over his mind until he becomes a slave to those desires and loses his freedom.**
> ...*John Milton's Paradise Lost*

---

[1] Allen, James, *The Life Triumphant,* ReadaClassic.com, p.16
[2] The Great Courses, PC445 3, *Natural Law and Human Nature*, p. 17
[3] www.JosephsonInstitute.org
[4] Allen, James, *The Life Triumphant,* ReadaClassic.com.
[5] Eben Alexander, *Proof of Heaven*, Simon & Shuster, NY, p.85

Chapter 4

The Pharaoh's Treasure

After dinner, Carter asks Claire if she would like to go for a walk. She says she would love to, and they are soon walking in the woods along a beautiful rippling mountain creek on a warm evening.

Carter shares the team's concern that Doc is way overworked, and that Warden is turning away dying patients. Other patients who manage to get on the six-month waiting list are dying before they can be seen he says.

We think the best solution would be to bring on a trainee to learn Doc's methods and assume some of the workload. Doc wants someone with basic medical training, but not so much that he or she is not open to alternative healing options.

Carter remarks as casually as he can, "Didn't you first come to meet Doc because you were interested in alternative medicine?"

"Well, sure, I am interested in reasonably alternative medicine but not just anything like witchcraft, leeches or bleeding people," she replies trying to sound disinterested.

"Oh, well, gee, weren't all of those a part of traditional medicine at one time?" he asks.

They look at each other and burst out laughing, knowing that neither is fooling the other. "Well, I can't speak for Doc," says Carter, "but would you be interested?"

"Of course, I would," she replies. "I would have to talk it over with my parents and consider the potential impact on my medical studies and stuff, but you can bet I am very much interested in the possibility."

For a long while, they sit by the river, and at one-point Claire says, "You know the Doctor has an excellent reputation as an extraordinarily gifted surgeon and practitioner of his original specialty, neurology, not to mention all he has learned since about alternative medicine. I wonder what else he can do and how he does it?"

"Well, I do know he uses a fair amount of experimental drug compounds including many that we make here from a host of natural ingredients and controlled substances that I have to document. Other than that, I don't know what he does with patients or how he cures them. You know doctors from all over refer their toughest cases to him," says Carter.

Carter is also concerned that the pressure of trying to schedule patients and telling some they can't be seen in time to save them is wearing heavily on Warden.

He recalls that when they were Ascetics together, Warden missed his dog a great deal. Carter resolves to see if the farm property around Warden's house can be fenced in so Warden can have a dog, if he wants to because it would likely help relieve some of the stress.

Warden is thrilled with the idea of getting a dog and reminds Carter that pets are great stress reducers. Once they have the fence up, they go to the local dog pound to save an animal that is on "death row" as Warden calls it.

Warden can't make up his mind about which dog to save and which to let die. They end up bringing home a tan and white Collie named Buddy, a great black and white King Collie named Rebel, a German Shepherd named Barry, and a beautiful black and white Shepherd and Collie mix named Lady.

Chapter 4 The Pharaoh's Treasure

After worrying all night about a dog he left behind, Warden goes back the next day and liberates a brown Doberman named Bett, plus a pair of twin Lab and Shepherd mixes named Torrie and Jade and another Collie named Gabby for a total of eight large dogs.

"I might have overdone it a little," says Warden once all the dogs are home, and the garage is full of 50-pound bags of dry dog food.

"Do ya think?" replies Carter humorously.

Carter is quite happy for his friend, whose stress level really is much lower after his place becomes an animal farm. After all, if one pet will lower stress, imagine what eight will do. One thing eight dogs do is keep Warden busy with a pooper-scooper.

Carter and Claire agree that he would float her name as a possible trainee with Doc. Meanwhile, she will have time to think about it. Only if she wants to join the team and Doc is receptive, will she discuss it with her parents who are helping her pay for medical school.

It does not take much help from Carter to get Doc to see Claire as a potentially perfect trainee. Her high school and college were essentially pre-med, and she had passed her first year of medical school with flying colors. She is interested in alternative medicine and seems to fit in with the team perfectly.

Doc had already discussed the opportunity with Ashley and Mia, however, both are happy doing what they are doing and neither plans to become a doctor.

With Carter's encouragement, Claire goes home to talk the proposition over with her parents. Unexpectedly, her mom Brittany is against it and her dad Ryan, a physician himself, supports it. After a couple of days with no progress, Claire calls for reinforcements.

A man can be compelled to do anything, but his soul cannot be forced.
...Author Simon Soloveitchik, "Parenting for Everyone"

Carter decides to visit for the weekend to help Claire and finds Doc going with him. "Perhaps her mom will feel better about us, remarks Doc, once she sees that we are not Dr. Jeckle and Mr. Hyde." Both men are dressed in their Sunday best, and they have a great visit with Claire and her parents.

When they get back to base camp, Claire calls and says her mom is good for a one-year trial if the Dean of the Medical school will agree to give her a year's sabbatical. In fact, the Dean suggests she take some courses online, and he even offers her a directed study medical research course in alternative medicine if Doc will agree to teach Claire.

All is wrapped up in a month, and Claire is officially on board as a medical trainee to help Doc. Everyone is pleased, especially Carter.

Doc, watched closely by Claire, is trying to save the life of an older man in his seventies. He is a famous archeologist named Dr. Jones who has come down with an unexplained illness that has left him unable to speak and unable to move his head, arms, hands or fingers. It is rumored that he is under an ancient curse for unearthing the tomb of King Narmer, the first pharaoh of the first dynasty of Egypt.

The period of history covering the earliest Egyptian Dynasties is known as the Old Kingdom, and it extends back over 5,000 years. The Pharaohs of Egypt kept good records for their times including a complete listing of all the Kings that preceded them. But, much of the history of the first pharaoh will be forever shrouded in mystery.

However, Egyptian hieroglyphs of the middle kingdom era suggest that important, ancient secrets to human life known as the "Book of Living" had existed way back around the formation of the first imperial dynasty. Unfortunately, it has since been lost somewhere in the eons of time, and Dr. Jones has been searching for it.

Dr. Jones is trying to communicate something of great urgency, but since he could neither speak nor write, he is making little progress. Doc is stumped as to what is paralyzing the famous archeologist.

Carter and Claire devise a way to communicate with the frustrated patient by having him blink once for yes and twice for no. They have to

Chapter 4 The Pharaoh's Treasure

say or draw things they guess might be part of what he wants to say, which takes a while. They finally resort to pointing to each letter of the alphabet until he is able to spell out the words "Treasure Room."

Needless to say, these words elicit a great deal of interest. Things move a little faster after Jones spells out "King Narmer," which Carter quickly researches on his computer. King Narmer was the first Pharaoh to conquer Upper and Lower Egypt and unify them into one country. Narmer, like the following pharaohs of the first dynasty, is buried at the sacred city of Abydos 70 miles north-west of Egypt's famous Valley of the Kings where there are 63 royal Egyptian tombs.

As was the case with most Royal tombs in Egypt, tomb robbers had looted and destroyed King Narmer's tomb many centuries ago. However, Jones had recently found a false floor in the empty tomb below which is the real burial chamber containing Narmer's stone sarcophagus (stone body shaped coffin) and the dust of his bones. It is upon opening the sarcophagus that Dr. Jones becomes afflicted.

This last bit of information causes Doc to think maybe Jones had some kind of allergic shock to his nervous system in reaction to inhaling a bit of the 5,000-year-old dust of the first pharaoh's remains. He hopes injecting into Jones' bloodstream a bit of that same dust mixed with one of Doc's natural cocktails might bring relief to their impatient patient.

They decide to take the eminent archeologist back to Egypt to Narmer's burial chamber to see if enough uncontaminated dust remains to do the job. Doc also feels that being in the same location where the anaphylactic shock first took place might help to reverse it.

Carter takes care of the paperwork, visas and permits required to get Doc, Claire, Jones and himself into the royal tomb. The task is made much easier because Jones still has a valid permit from the Egyptian Bureau of Antiquities to explore the tomb.

> **A happy person is not a person in a certain set of circumstances, but rather a person in a certain set of attitudes.**
> *... Anonymous*

Once at the ancient burial ground of the pharaohs at Abydos, they get directions to the correct tomb. Although, they attempt to keep Jones' return to Egypt quiet, they are met with waiting news crews and cameras. Also, present is Dr. Julian Friarson, the heavyset Egyptian Minister of Antiquities dressed in the khaki uniform of an archeologist.

Dr. Friarson welcomes them and comments that he is glad to see two such famous doctors together at Abydos. In media interviews, Doc explains how they are going to attempt to resolve Dr. Jones' condition.

The four and Dr. Friarson descend a passageway of steep steps into the first level of the tomb. It is completely empty except for a couple of very dangerous Egyptian Cobras that retreat into the darkest corners of the chamber. Lanterns reveal walls of the burial chamber that are extensively decorated with colorful, exotic images of ancient Egyptian life.

They find the opening Dr. Jones made into the lower chamber and drop through five thousand years of history into the real burial chamber of the first pharaoh of Egypt. The ceiling is low, and the room is cool and dry just as Jones and his assistants left it. "Fortunately, someone has replaced the heavy lid of the stone sarcophagus probably in fear of its curse carrying contents!" jokes Doc.

Claire and Carter are in awe of the tomb, being captivated by the history of it all, for they are looking back to the very dawn of human civilization. While Doc is busy getting a treatment ready to infuse with Narmer's dust, everyone else slips on dust masks.

"Let's carefully slide the heavy lid of the sarcophagus ajar just enough to draw out some dust," says Doc.

Doc soon has a very thankful Dr. Jones back to normal except for some very sore muscles and a pounding headache. Once the euphoria of his cure subsides, Jones picks up a pickaxe he had left on his last visit.

"Egyptian Royal Tombs," says the archeologist, "often had a treasure room of valuable things the pharaoh considered important enough to take with him to the next world."

Chapter 4 The Pharaoh's Treasure

In the treasure rooms of the middle and late kingdoms, there had been gold and silver of great wealth. Most had been stolen by tomb robbers in past centuries, but tombs that had been found undisturbed like the one we are in now contained fabulous riches.

Jones adds, "Behind the back wall of the burial chamber is the most likely location for a sealed treasure vault." After carefully digging at the back wall for a while, Dr. Jones sits down and adds, "Since this is the tomb of the very first pharaoh, it may not be arranged as were the later tombs."

Noticing that the older man is out of breath, Carter asks if he might give it a try. Jones looks at the Minister of Antiquities who nods his approval. After about 10 minutes of careful digging, Carter feels the wall give way and he falls forward with part of the dusty wall onto the floor of the hidden room. It also gives way as a trap door drops him down a steep chute into another chamber.

Carter quickly realizes that wherever he is, he is not alone, as he can hear many voices speaking in some kind of ancient or primitive sounding language. His eyes begin to adjust to the fire light in the room, and he realizes he is laying on a narrow rock ledge witnessing some kind of very important ceremony just below him.

"I can't believe this," thinks Carter, as he lay flat, face down, where he has fallen, too afraid to move or hardly breathe. "They don't realize I am here. This looks like some kind of tribunal with maybe forty small participants seated in a semicircle. All of them are richly dressed in ancient Egyptian attire doing a great deal of jabbering."

The assembly's focus seems to be on a large, ornate scale with round gold trays suspended by silver threads at either end of a horizontal, gold cross bar. The cross bar is supported in the center by a tall, heavily engraved, silver, support column anchored in a gold base. Both trays are empty so the scale is in perfect balance, and it seems to be attended by a boy with the head of a fox.

**A professional is someone who can do his best work
even when he doesn't feel like it."**
...Alistair Cooke

A Soul's Code of Conduct

The whole scene is illuminated by a great fire pit with flames reaching high into the air causing shifting shadows on walls covered in colorful Egyptian hieroglyphics. The air smells of incense, and Carter senses that something big is about to take place.

A tall, skinny, stylishly dressed man with the head of a jackal approaches the scale, leading an older, obviously worried Egyptian man in white robes. As the man is led toward the scale, Carter hears people murmuring the name Narmer!

Carter then notices approaching from the opposite direction, a richly dressed man in a golden robe seated in a carriage carried by four elegant female attendants. The gathered assembly stands chanting the name "Osiris", as he is carried in with great fanfare. The carriage is lowered and Osiris moves gracefully to a tall black and gold throne facing the scale as if to observe or judge whatever is about to happen.

"Good grief how gruesome," thinks Carter as an ugly beast with the head of a crocodile, the front legs and body of a lion and the back legs of a fat hippopotamus moves up and sits drooling near the scale.

The crowd has quieted, tension is building and Carter is sweating profusely when from somewhere above, a radiantly shimmering silver feather slowly descends onto one of the scale's golden trays, tipping the balance ever so slightly. The observers in unison begin to speak in a slow reverent voice repeating the word Ma-at.

An eerie silence falls over the scene, and the anticipation is intense. The fox-headed boy approaches Narmer and slowly moves an open hand across Narmer's head and chest. As he does so, what appears to be Narmer's soul comes forth and moves onto the scale's other golden tray opposite the feather of Maat.

Ever so slowly, the scale comes into balance, and there is an obvious sigh of relief from Narmer as his soul returns to his body. A man with the head of a hawk steps forth writes something on a tablet then leads Narmer over to the regal Osiris who touches each of his shoulders with a gold Egyptian scepter, and Narmer appears to evaporate.

Chapter 4 The Pharaoh's Treasure

"I can't believe what I'm seeing," thinks Carter. Then a beautifully dressed, stunning and exotic woman, perhaps one of Narmer's wives, is led unwillingly to the great scale. The process is the same only this time the scale tilts out of balance because her soul is heavier than the feather.

In a flash, the ugly crocodile headed beast leaps up and gobbles down the woman's soul, and immediately as it does so, her body turns to dust. Carter puts his head down on his arms in shock, thinking what an ugly end it is to such a beautiful woman.

Then Carter freezes as he feels a snake moving across the back of his legs and up his back! Still face down on his stomach where he'd fallen, but now paralyzed with fear, he prays hard that it's not a deadly Egyptian Cobra. He feels it move over the back of his neck then slowly it slithers down his shoulder and around in front of his frozen face.

"It's it's a rope, it's just a rope! It's not a snake! Oh, thank God it's just a rope," thinks Carter with extreme relief. A smooth woven leather rope has a note attached reading "tie this around you and we will pull you up."

Looking back toward the fiery scene, Carter now sees nothing but darkness, so he quickly ties the rope around himself and gives it a tug. Slowly, they pull him back up the chute and through the open trap door where he is greeted heartily by his friends.

"Are you ok?" asks Claire with concern. "That was a long fall, and you seemed to be out of it for several minutes."

With our flashlights, we could see you lying at the bottom of the chute, but you didn't respond to our calls, says Dr. Jones adding, "I am sure glad it wasn't me that went through that trap door for I doubt I could have survived the fall so well."

> **"You don't believe in the soul
> until you feel it straining to escape the body."**
> *...Author Glen Duncan, in a Day and a Night and a Day*

A Soul's Code of Conduct

"Well," thinks Carter, "I am not sure I survived it so well either." Carter goes on to explain what he witnessed. Jones quickly asks if he has ever seen the Egyptian Book of the Dead. Carter replied that he has heard of it but never seen it. That's absolutely incredible says Jones. What you have described in perfect detail is exactly what is depicted in an ancient book you have never seen.

When asked what it all means, Jones explains that Carter described the "Weighing of the Soul" ceremony. The ancient Egyptians believed that when they died their souls, conditioned by their behavior on earth, would be judged to determine if they would be allowed to enter the next dimension of existence, which they called the "Afterlife."

The ceremony was always performed in front of Osiris, the chief god of the afterlife and a tribunal of 42 other lesser deities. The great scale would weigh the dead person's soul against the feather of Maat, the symbol of truth and justice. If their soul balanced with the feather, the person was saved and Osiris would transmute them to the Afterlife.

If the soul was heavier with the weight of sin and wrongdoing, the scale would not balance and the soul would be devoured by the ugly beast Ammit "the gobbler." Once a person's soul was devoured, that person ceased to exist whispered Jones in his raspy voice.

I simply cannot imagine how in the world you could have seen or even dreamed of it in such perfect detail. It is just incredible, says Jones. You must have been knocked unconscious by the fall and had some kind of vision brought on by our location or the trap door.

Well, I do have a knot on my head, says Carter, but it all seemed so vivid and so real, much more so even than a dream. I was completely awestruck and terrified at the same time.

Doc asks Carter how Narmer's soul appeared when it moved from Narmer's body to the scale.

"The soul becomes dyed with the color of its thoughts."
...Roman Emperor Marcus Aurelius

Chapter 4 The Pharaoh's Treasure

Carter says it seemed at first to be a faint, full sized shadow of his body, however it flashed into an iridescent star like the Star of Bethlehem then it reduced into a small vessel on the scale roughly in the shape of a human heart.

The reverse occurred when the soul returned to his body, says Carter. It expanded from the heart, flashed as a star and changed back into a faint, full color shadow of his body, which was quickly re-absorbed therein. "Can we send a team down there to see if there are any signs of what I saw?" asks Carter.

"We sure will," says Dr. Jones, "But first, let's get back into that treasure room and see what the first Pharaoh of Egypt thought was worth more than anything else on earth."

The thin, gray haired Jones cautiously pulls a loose part of the wall back into the burial chamber to keep it from falling on anything inside the treasure room. Avoiding the trap door, Jones using a small flashlight crawls inside the mysterious cavity as Friarson cautions him to, "Look out for snakes."

"Come on in and bring the lanterns," calls Jones from well within the small room.

As they enter the treasure room with light from the electric lanterns, they can see that they are in a small vault with a ceiling no more than five feet above a smooth floor.

Unfortunately, the room is empty except for a golden chest on an altar in the center of the room. Jones and Friarson approach the chest, and Jones says here there is a seal on the chest with an inscription that translates something like Tabula Vita or "Life Book."

"The Book of Living," exclaims the Minister of Antiquities. "There have been references to it in the writings of subsequent dynasties, but none of it has ever been found - until now," he says hopefully.

Don't curse the darkness, light a candle.
...Chinese proverb

A Soul's Code of Conduct

With great anticipation, Doc, Claire, Carter and Friarson crowd around, Jones as he carefully removes the ancient seal and slowly opens the gold chest. In it are two thick scrolls of papyrus paper covered in some kind of preservative. Jones tries to hide his disappointment over the lack of treasure, but he does realize the heavy chest itself must be solid gold. They close the chest and carefully carry it out of the tomb.

Jones says, "There must be something of great importance on those scrolls if old Narmer thought it was the most important thing he could take to the next life, more so even than all the riches of gold, silver and jewels he must have had at his disposal."

The exploration of the chamber Carter had fallen into reveals no evidence of what he had seen other than faded hieroglyphics on the walls. On the way home, Carter asks Doc what he makes of Carter's unusual vision.

Doc replies that just as we have today, many civilizations had belief systems that posited a relationship between human conduct on earth and the destination or condition of life after death.

What you saw in your vision was most likely the result of your fall, your spiritually sensitive mind, your vivid imagination and our five-thousand-year-old location. We know such composite creatures like the "Gobbler" and men with animal heads could not exist. However, the basic premise that human conduct on earth affects the destination or condition of life after death is certainly sound and your description of Narmer's soul fits well with what I know.

Once back in the U.S., Dr. Jones translates the scrolls and gives a copy to Doc in appreciation for saving his life. Jones tells Doc that besides Carter's vision, another mystery of this episode is that at the time of Narmer's death the Egyptians had not yet developed the kind of fully written language used in the scrolls they recovered, and they would not do so for another 500 years. This left Jones wondering about possibly divine sources for the "Book of Living" and a renewed interest in the search for the rest of it.

Chapter 4 The Pharaoh's Treasure

Doc gives the translated text to Carter who conducts additional research on its main concepts and themes and updates it to make it relevant to the 21st century. Thinking about the value of the scrolls, Carter recalls hearing that when you leave this world it is not only the condition of your soul that counts, but perhaps important also is what you leave behind to help those who come after you.

Thinking about that, Carter realizes that even after five thousand years, Narmer, the first Pharaoh of Egypt, has with those scrolls left humanity exceedingly valuable insights into the development of the human soul. In fact, Carter finds it to be so valuable in a practical sense that he includes it in the Handbook of the Soul that he, Warden and the Colonel are keeping for their future descendants. Carter and Claire also offer to use it for the monthly seminar as presented on the following pages:

**Everyone's soul is immortal,
but those of the righteous are both immortal and divine.**
...Socrates, Father of Philosophy

Handbook of the Soul
Attitude

I. Preview

It is critically important to have a positive attitude because of the difference it can make in the progress of your soul and in the enjoyment of this life.

1. You and you alone are responsible for your attitude.
2. The first step to improve our attitudes is to manage what we allow into our minds.

II. Introduction

Carter and Clair explain that the important concepts they are about to present are based in part on wisdom found in the five- thousand-year-old scrolls of the "Book of Living". They also explain how they came to have the ancient material and what wisdom it must have represented to the first Egyptian Pharaoh.

- Carter begins by reminding everyone that part of human life is about overcoming challenges and solving problems.
- Approaching life's challenges with a negative attitude greatly **reduces** the chances we will find the best solution. However, a positive attitude significantly **increases** the odds you will find the best solution.

A professional attitude is a positive attitude that says we can do this, solve this, fix this, sell this or resolve this and just let us at it!

That is a powerful, professional attitude and an empowered person with such an attitude is much more likely to find good solutions than someone who fears that they might not be able to get it done.

So, today we're going to talk about how to establish that most important of the soul's qualities, a positive attitude, and how best to maintain and protect it.

We will discuss the following two objectives concerning a positive attitude:

1. **Importance** - We're going to discuss the critical importance of having a positive attitude.
2. **Improvement** - We will talk about three significant steps that we can take to improve our attitudes.

III. Importance of a Positive Attitude

A philosopher once said, that our lives are like checkbooks, and we have a certain lifetime account, and in that account, instead of dollars, we have maybe 36,000 days.

You can figure that if a person lives maybe 100 years, times 365 days a year, that long-lived person will have somewhere around 36,000 days in her checkbook of life.

- *Now, each time you write a check or "spend" it, that money is gone from your account, is it not?*
- *Every day you live is gone also from your account, and you'll never have it to live again.*
- *Now, pretty clearly, if we each had only $36,000 to make it all the way through life, we would probably be very careful to get the most benefit from each dollar.*

If you think about it, you likely have much less than 36,000 days remaining; how you spend them will greatly affect the character and quality of your eternal soul.

Someday, as your soul departs your body, you may look back on your life to evaluate how well you lived it, and how much your soul grew from the effort you put into improving it during your life.

More Impact - *The attitude of your soul has more impact on your life than anything else.*

- *It's very important to realize, as we have said before, that it doesn't matter so much what happens to you in life.*
- *What matters is how you **respond or react** to whatever happens to you. A primary driver that determines how you respond or react is your attitude.*

"Weakness of attitude becomes weakness of character."
...Nobel Laureate Albert Einstein

Surveys show that on the job, ten percent of people that are fired are fired for a negative attitude and many more for the results of a negative attitude.

Now some people are just naturally positive.

Then there are those people that just wake up in the morning in a bad mood.

In fact, did you hear about somebody asking one guy if he wakes up grouchy in the morning?

And he said, "Heck no. I let her sleep!"

"Hey," said Claire, "I thought that translated the other way around!"

IV. Attitude Improvement

Who do you think gets the worst of a person's bad attitude? Where does your true attitude come out?

"At home with the family and close friends," said Mia.

"Improving our attitudes might also add a few more days to our lives," said Laura.

There we go! That's right! Now, you put more life in your living and more living in your life and more life time in your lifetime! Moreover, you know excess stress just tears people up, and over a prolonged period, it definitely affects one's health.

"Therefore, I think most people would agree," said Carter, "that it really is a worthwhile effort to learn how to have a more positive attitude. Like the first Pharaoh, we might even consider it to be more valuable than diamonds or gold."

Laura asked, "What about someone who says, heck, what you're trying to tell me is that I should come to work and act happy even when I don't feel happy?"

"That's true," said Claire, "However, most people would rather work all day with someone that's acting happy, even if they're not happy, than to have to work with a sincere sorehead any day."

Chapter 4 The Pharaoh's Treasure

- *You should act reasonably happy and positive at work to help contribute to a positive professional atmosphere.*
- *People don't get paid to be negative on their jobs; they are paid to give their professional best.*

"That means not lowering the performance of their team, so acting positive and reasonably happy, if necessary, is the professional thing to do!" said Doc.

- *The professional thing to do is to carry your share of the load and contribute your share to a positive atmosphere at home and on the job without whining and griping about it.*
- *From the chapters on happiness, you may remember that one way to pull yourself out of a sour mood is to act as if you're in a happier state of mind.*

"Evidently, the secret here," said Carter, "is that acting positive and happy eventually seeps into your soul and contributes to your becoming more positive and happier."

Fake It - Make it - Sometimes, he added, you just have to "fake it until you make it."

"I wonder," asks Warden, "how long it takes to make a noticeable improvement in a person's attitude?"

"It probably depends on how negative the person is to start with," responds Claire, "but we do know the following about attitudes and time:"

- *An attitude is not something that changes daily. An attitude is something we develop over time.*
- *Moods can change frequently, but attitudes are built over an extended time frame.*
- *It usually takes about 30 days of continuous behavior to create a habit of that behavior.*
- *However, it may take a while before some people can get through 30 **continuous** days with a truly positive attitude.*

A Soul's Code of Conduct

"Who do you think has the most influence on your attitude at work?" asks Claire.

"I'd say your supervisor or your boss or it could also be customers, especially if you have irate, angry customers," says a temporary nurse.

So, you think it's your boss or your customers. Anyone else?

"Yourself," says Laura.

"Yep, that's the answer," replies Carter.

- On the job, it's the same as off the job.
- It's not the customers, the boss or even the difficult computers you may have to work with.
- At home, it's not the kids or your spouse unless your spouse is quite negative.

Nah! We can't blame it on the usual list of suspects. If you want to see who really establishes your attitude, just look in the mirror!

- We and we alone decide what our attitudes will be!
- Each of us controls his or her own attitude.
- If you want to develop a more positive attitude, you can't fool yourself and think it is someone else's fault that your attitude is negative.
- Remember, it's not what happens to us in life that matters; it's how we react to what happens to us.

Life is about how you respond positively or react negatively to everything else and everyone else in your life. Those choices are **yours to make** regardless of your genetic dispositions or anything else.

Constant exposure to negative people, including a toxic spouse or coworker, could have an impact on your attitude. However, you and you alone are responsible for what you pay attention to and what you let affect your attitude.

Chapter 4 The Pharaoh's Treasure

"Your attitude," says Claire "is essentially, what you develop and maintain as an outlook on life. It isn't going to change overnight based on the kind of customers you are dealing with or the boss you have, unless you have to sit right beside a toxic person all day.

"I'm not saying life isn't more pleasant with a good boss or a positive spouse, but your own attitude is very much a reflection of what is inside of you and how you choose to react to what happens to you."

*"If you are prepared to defend against negativity when exposed to it, it shouldn't affect your attitude too much unless you are exposed to it **continuously**.*

"For example, you might find yourself with dangerous levels of exposure to close family members, and close friends or co-workers with whom you spend a lot of time.

"We sure don't need somebody else's toxic attitude rubbing off on us. Nevertheless, we can determine who we let influence us, so it remains our choice."

"What do you think are some steps that people can take to improve their attitudes?" asks Claire.

Surprisingly, no one answers. Claire then lists the following:

- *Communications going **into** your mind based on what you listen to, read and watch affect your attitude.*
- *Things, which you frequently choose to think about and **dwell on in your mind** greatly affect your attitude.*
- *Communications **from** your mind, which you control.*

The greatest discovery of my generation is that human beings can alter their lives by altering their attitudes of mind.
...20th century Psychologist William James

*The **first** thing that can affect your attitude is what you listen to, read and watch. You don't want to become a willing receptacle for the foul, negative garbage that some other people are putting out. In this age of computers, we know that if you put garbage in to a computer you get what out?*

"If you put garbage in, you get garbage out," said a young patient named Rebekah who was staying a while at the base camp.

In many ways, our minds are like super computers: garbage in, garbage out. If you keep feeding negative input into the mind of your soul with what you read, watch or listen to, what do you think is going to come out?

"Obviously, the negative," said Doc matter-of-factly.

Exactly! On the other hand, if you keep feeding yourself with positives, then positives are going to shape your attitude.

- *After all, you can control what you hear.*
- *You can remove yourself, and not hang around with negative people.*
- *Alternatively, you can tell them, "Hey, I'd just as soon not talk about so much negativity."*
- *If you did, people would pause and think twice before they talked negatively around you again.*
- *Most people just don't realize the impact of their negative thinking and downbeat conversation.*
- *Just realize that each of them is pouring a little poison into your life each time they engage in cynicism and negativity.*

Much of the pessimism probably comes from the news media. It's an unfortunate fact that negative, sensational news is of much more interest to people than positive news and uplifting information.

It's not just what you see, but how you look at it.
...Unknown

Chapter 4 The Pharaoh's Treasure

- *Therefore, people in the news media have to make a living reporting on the most negative news they can find.*
- *Cable and satellite news channels with 24 hour-a-day news coverage can be overwhelming.*
- *It seems as though we've been living through decades of national negativity.*

Continuous exposure to the news and other negative input over time will affect your attitude.

Unfortunately, we have institutionalized the negative to such an extent that **half the population is now taking anti-depressant medication.** *It's insane; it's attitude suicide; and over time, it can have such a dramatic effect on our lives, our families and our souls.*

All the information that's coming into your mind is leaving an impression within you, so, what might an attitude x-ray of your soul reveal?

- *You could* ***choose*** *to read some good positive uplifting material.*
- *If you drive to work, you can play some good positive, motivational material and listen to something inspirational.*
- *You can take control and feed yourself good, positive things while reducing the amount of negativity coming in.*

You can be adequately informed of the important news and events of the day by listening to fewer than 15 minutes of headline news reporting each day.

"There's some fantastic material out there in an endless variety of formats. Just enter "motivational books" or "positive attitude" in your computer's search engine. Some of the material is really funny and you might even try something spiritual for it is mostly uplifting as well," said Carter.

You choose to whom and to what you expose your mind. Therefore, the first step is to be aware of the kinds of programming you are allowing into you're the mind of your soul.

A Soul's Code of Conduct

You'd be surprised at what can happen when you get more positive material flowing into your mind. When you have a goal, a purpose and you feed your mind positively, you could see a much more positive attitude emerge.

- Research has shown that a positive attitude can add years to our lives.[1]
- A 30-year study of 447 people at the Mayo Clinic found that optimists had around a 50 percent lower risk of early death than pessimists.[2]
- A Yale study of 660 seniors concluded that elderly people with the most positive attitude about aging lived an average of 7.5 years longer than those with the most negative attitudes.[3]
- A Dutch study examined the attitudes and longevity of 999 people over the age of 65. The study reported that people with a positive attitude lived longer and had a 77 percent lower risk of heart disease than pessimists.[4]

Constant worry is like a stream of fear that slowly cuts a channel of apprehension through your mind, until it becomes a raging river of anxious, fearful thought that can dominate the mind of your soul.[5]

V. Summary

Carter and Claire conclude by summarizing part I as follows:

1. We talked about the critical importance of having a positive attitude and the big difference it can make in the enjoyment and length of life. More importantly, it is a key factor in the overall development of your soul.
2. We noted that you and you alone are responsible for your attitude.
3. We discussed the first significant step we can take to improve our attitudes, which is by controlling what we allow into our minds.

Our attitude towards life determines life's attitude towards us.
...*Motivational Speaker Earl Nightingale*

Chapter 4 The Pharaoh's Treasure

*In the next chapter, we will continue to examine a Positive Attitude. We will begin with the **second way** we can affect our attitudes.*

According to *THE POINT DENVER BLOG,* Ten steps to a more optimistic attitude include:[6]

"1) **Practice Gratitude** - A grateful mindset exerts a powerful influence on your outlook. Not only does it make you feel good in the moment, it also shifts your focus in a positive direction and reduces your concern about anything that you may be lacking.

"2) **Embrace Happiness** - Being happy is not about circumstances or any other outside force. Happiness is a decision we make. Why not make up your mind to embrace happiness, instead of worry. Worrying is just tormenting oneself with disturbing thoughts.

"3) **Replace Problems with Challenges** - Subconsciously, the word "problem" says, 'Life is not as it should be'. Seeing an experience as challenge will focus our attention on a positive outcome.

"4) **Enjoy the Journey** - A journey is an adventure of discovery. When we are on a journey, we don't fear change; we welcome it. We look forward to new and unfamiliar experiences. On a journey, we are full of optimism because we are filled with the expectation of a wonderful adventure. This is the perfect attitude to carry with you every day.

"5) **Take Time to Smell the Roses** - When you constantly feel rushed and scattered, it can be difficult to maintain an optimistic outlook. By pausing briefly to really taste your food or enjoy a beautiful piece of music, you remind yourself of the joy of simplicity.

"6) **Start the Day on a Positive Note** - Find a few minutes each morning to clear your mind and then think positive thoughts about the upcoming day. Focus on the people and events that bring you joy or a sense of satisfaction. Then carry that feeling with you all day long."

Doubt kills more dreams than failure ever will!

"7) Treasure Hunt - Make it a habit to actively search for the positive side of everything. With practice, you will be surprised how easy it becomes to see the not so obvious benefits and pleasures all around you.

"8) Act Happy - You can use words and body language to program your nervous system. When you make a conscious effort to walk the walk and talk the talk, your feelings will soon follow. If you act like an optimistic person, your mind accepts that as your reality. Try it and see for yourself.

"9) Keep Company with Positive People - The attitude of the people around us can be a powerful force for good or bad. Seek out the company of those with a sunny disposition and let yourself be influenced by their optimism.

"10) Do A Nightly Gratitude Review - Before you go to bed think of at least three things for which you are truly grateful. Let yourself feel the joy that those things bring to your life. Think about what you could have done a little differently that day perhaps to share the joy and gratitude with other people."

Owing to the continuing shortages of everything in the Socialist American economy and the lack of animal protein in our diets, we have smuggled a pair of goats, a pair of chickens and a rooster into the country from some of Doc's former patients abroad. The idea is to breed them and raise our own animals.

In addition to food riots, there are now incidents of roving gangs stealing and robbing food from farmers. The government keeps a lid on such stories and the news media is not allowed to report on them because they are considered anti-socialist. With the government in control of the press, it is hard to know what is really going on. The truth has become as scarce as food and most of the news sounds like propaganda.

> "The eyes are the windows of the soul."
> ...Ancient philosopher PLATO, in Phaedrus

Chapter 4 The Pharaoh's Treasure

There are several clandestine radio stations that say some starving people are eating their pets and that mobs have even broken into zoos killing the animals for food. We have begun taking precautions for our own safety and the protection of our animals.

> **"Here's death twitching in my ear;**
> **"Live well," says he, "for I am coming."**
> *...Ancient Poet Virgil*

Engraved Nile River Scene

A Soul's Code of Conduct

Egyptian depiction of the weighing of the soul against the Feather of Truth

**1920s silent movie star Charlie Chaplin said,
"Restraint of tempers, appetites, bad habits, and so on is
a mighty good thing to cultivate."**

---

[1] http://www.huffingtonpost.com/david-r-hamilton-phd/positive-people-live-long_b_774648.html
[2] Toshihiko Maruta, Robert C. Colligan, Michael Malinchoc, Kenneth P. Offord; Mayo Clinic Proceedings, Vol. 75, Issue 2, p140–143 February, 2000
[3] Levy, Slade, Kunkel, And Kasl - Journal of Personality and Social Psychology, 2002, Vol. 83, No.2 261–270 Copyright 2002 by the American Psychological Association, Inc.
[4] Erik J. Giltay, MD et al; JAMA Psychiatry, Vol 61, No. 11 November 2004 Arch Gen Psychiatry 2004; 61 (11):1126-1135. doi:10.1001/archpsyc.61.11.1126
[5] From a sermon by Pastor Harold Massey, 22 May 2016
[6] http://www.thepointdenver.com/blog/2012/01/11

Chapter 5
Attitude of the Soul

Hi, I am Carter, and I will be your personal guide in this chapter. Many doctors and other skilled medical professionals are leaving the country every day creating a major health care crisis. Under Socialism, we have "Medicare for All," except that there are no longer enough doctors for all. Our patients tell us there are long, long lines at the hospitals and clinics that are still open, with people camping outside in line for days waiting to be seen.

In our little mountain valley, we are trying to stay more or less out of the news so the government won't notice us. However, with the doctor shortage, sick and injured people are also camping out along the road to our base camp waiting to see Doc and that is bringing unwanted attention from the government.

It has been a month since the last seminar, and the team has been working hard using the interactive video system to help nurses and EMTs across the country who are trying to do the work of doctors. Claire is proving to be an able and insightful student of both traditional and alternative medicine, and both Doc and Claire are working longer each day trying to keep up with the lengthening lines of patients

At our invitation, my mom, Casey, and my grandfather, the Colonel, have come to visit. They get the full story of the trip to Egypt at dinner Friday, and after dinner, Claire and I present the second half of the seminar about the Attitude of the Soul, which goes as follows:

Chapter 5 Attitude of the Soul

Handbook of the Soul

Attitude

I. Review of Part 1 - (from the last chapter)

Welcome to the second half of the seminar on the importance of a positive attitude. As a quick review, the following are the four major points from the first part of the seminar:

1. It is critically important to have a positive attitude because it is a key factor in the progress of your soul and in the enjoyment of life.

2. You and you alone are responsible for your attitude.

3. The first significant step to improving and protecting our attitudes is to **manage the information coming into our minds, so that you read, watch and hear mostly good stuff.**

4. Subject yourself to very few negative or critical influences.

II. Preview part 2

Our minds are the battlegrounds where positive and negative thoughts are fighting for control of our souls. Human life is an opportunity to develop the eternal qualities of your soul, especially your attitude because it is the core and tone of your being.

1. Take control over the things, which you frequently think about and dwell on in your mind and replace stinking thinking with the good stuff; visualize your success.

2. Take control over the kinds of things you talk about. Put a guard on your mouth and avoid speaking negatively!

III. Attitude Improvement

As previously noted, the **first** way to improve your attitude is to control what comes into your mind. The **second way** we can change our attitudes is with the **things we think about**; with the thoughts we entertain and maintain in our minds.

<u>**Popping In**</u> - You cannot always control every thought that pops into your mind. Have you ever noticed that you can be going along thinking about one thing, and a fearful thought jumps up in your mind?

Sometimes, negative thoughts jump in, but the **key point** is that although you cannot always control the thoughts that pop into your thinking, you **can control** the thoughts you **retain** in your conscious mind.

- You **can control** what you choose to **dwell upon** or **think about**.
- If negative things are coming into your mind, just do not retain them.
- Don't think about problems; think about solutions.
- You have the power within your mind to toss the negative out and pick up another positive train of thought.

Speaking on this topic, a wise man once said thoughts are like birds: you can't keep birds from flying over your head, but you can sure keep them from nesting in your hair. We can just as surely keep negative thoughts from nesting in our minds.

For instance, in your mind, count from one to ten. While you are counting, say your whole name. You could not say your name and keep counting at the same time.

- *We cannot maintain both thoughts at the same time.*
- *You had to stop the numbering sequence until you finished saying your name.*
- *Then you brought it back in your mind to finish the count.*
- *Therefore, you clearly have control over what you choose to keep in your mind.*

When we're constantly engaged in stinking thinking, it puts our attitudes on diets of negativity.

- *We can choose to replace negative thoughts with positive ones.*
- *It will be a constant battle for a while, until your mind becomes conditioned to positive thinking.*
- *Don't dwell on negative thoughts. They'll eat you alive.*

In his book "How Champions Think," Bob Rotella notes that in sports and in life, exceptional people **choose** their attitudes, and they **choose** to be exceptional.

<u>Not Blank</u> - When you're worrying about something negative, you can put it out of your mind, but it's going to try to get right back in.

- *You must move it right back out, saying, oh, no, you don't!*
- *The critical step is to substitute positive or creative thinking in its place.*
- *Our minds cannot stay blank, and they will revert to whatever kinds of thinking they are used to unless we intervene.*
- *Over time, it will get easier as your mind adjusts to positive instead of negative thinking.*

Since some kind of thinking is always going on while we are conscious and awake, we need to make sure it is mostly positive thinking.

- *This does not mean ignoring problems.*

- *It means once problems are identified and understood, we should concentrate our thinking on solutions to remedy the problems. Then take appropriate action.*

- *We cannot resolve problems by complaining and talking them to death.*

- *When fighting negative thoughts, we can think about and appreciate the good people and things we have in our lives.*

- *We can have pre-planned, positive topics to push in when negativity and worry are trying to take control.*

- *There's a direct parallel between positive thinking and a positive attitude.*

The term **thoughtform** refers to the fact that thoughts are energy in pre-physical form. If positive or negative thoughts occur with enough frequency and emotion, they can physically manifest accordingly in positive or negative ways.[1]

- *Interestingly enough, that's why busy people, who stay active doing something, are less often the gripers and complainers.*

- *Because those that are busy working to accomplish something have their attention and their energies focused on a positive goal instead of the critical, destructive purposes of finding fault.*

- *They have their minds employed on something active and positive, so they have better things to do with their time than using it to gossip, worry and find fault.*

Thus, we have a great deal of control over the **following two factors** that shape our attitudes.

1. The information we **accept into our mind** via conversation, media and music, etc.

2. The kinds of things we **dwell on** and think about most of the time

Chapter 5 Attitude of the Soul

Eventually, our outlooks on life and the health of our souls are also affected by that which affects our attitudes.

Let's cover a little about thought and purpose. At work, you have a purpose; you are there to do whatever you are being paid to do. If you don't know what that is, you need to find out fast.

The brilliant nineteenth century British philosopher James Allen wrote:[2]

- Having determined their purpose, people should mentally mark out a straight pathway to its achievement looking to neither the right nor left.
- "Doubts and fears should be rigorously excluded; they are disintegrating elements which break up the straight line of effort, rendering it crooked, weak and less effective."
- Thoughts of doubt and fear never accomplish anything except to lead to failure.
- Purpose, energy, the power to do and reason are disrupted when doubt and fear creep in.

Dorothy Hulst transcribed Allen noting that[3]

- The will 'to do' springs in part from the knowledge that we can do. Doubt and fear are the great enemies of this knowledge.
- They that encourage doubt and fear (or do not reject them), thwart themselves at every step.
- She who has mastered doubt and fear has largely conquered failure. Her every thought is allied with power, and difficulties are bravely met and wisely overcome.

A Soul's Code of Conduct

- *Thought allied courageously to purpose becomes creative force; those who realize this are ready to become something greater than a measly bundle of wavering thoughts and fluctuating sensations.*

- *She, who conquers misgiving and anxiety, becomes the intelligent wielder of the great spiritual authority and mental power available from within her soul (from God).*

Now, let's look at the **third factor** that affects our attitudes, which is **what we say**. The words we choose to speak.

The thoughts in your mind have an effect on your attitude and its development, but when you translate those thoughts into the words you choose to speak, it has an even greater impact on your **attitude.**

- What you say has a powerful impact because you've taken the thoughts in your mind and affirmed or reaffirmed them by proclaiming them in your own words.

- You are passing them along to others with your own signature of endorsement attached.

- Therefore, what you say has the strongest impact on you, your attitude and the nature of your outlook on life.

Again, this takes place over time. What you think about and say in any one day will not determine your attitude for that day. However, continued thought and speech **over time** begins to form and shape your attitude around the predominate nature of your thought and speech.

Once your thinking and conversation have been mostly positive for 30 days or so, it begins to have a noticeable impact on your attitude.

It's very much like exercising your muscles. You can't go to the gym and start doing curls with weights and think you're going to have some nice big biceps after the first or second day.

> **"Pleasant words are as a honeycomb, sweet to the soul, and health to the bones."**
> ...*Proverbs 16:24*

Chapter 5 Attitude of the Soul

- *Bodybuilders know it can take weeks or months to get on a good regimen and develop a strong body from working out.*
- *We're talking effective change but not instant change.*
- *You have to consider the kinds of things you have been reading, watching, hearing, thinking and talking about for the last six months or more to understand what is affecting your attitude today.*
- *Negative in, Negative out! Positive in, Positive out!*

Most any subject you want to consider has a negative side and a positive side. If you're talking about a problem at work, then you need to discuss the problem enough so your team understands what needs to be solved.

- *Then you want to start talking about the solutions.*
- *If we would talk solutions to our problems instead of dwelling on the problem, we would find that the solutions would come about more easily.*
- *We would become solution minded.*

Take for instance a ball team, let's say you have the world champion baseball team playing in the World Series, and it's the New York Yankees playing the L.A. Dodgers.

When one team is out on the field, they're certainly not out there saying to the pitcher and talking to each other saying negative things like the following:

- *Oh no, this guy's going to hit a home run!*
- *We're going to lose it in this inning.*
- *I can't see how we're going to win this one.*
- *Oh man, this team is really tough.*
- *I sure hope you guys are awake.*
- *I feel terrible over here on second base.*
- *Toss that ball over here; let me make sure I can hold on to it.*

- *I'm going to drop it for sure even if I do catch it.*

It's hard to imagine a team out there talking negatively like that. You will never see that in any major league sport because they know that what they say affects their mindset and performance.

If you have ever played football softball, baseball, any kind of team sport, you will recall that the coaches no doubt emphasized the importance of a winning attitude.

Baseball coaches tell us they want to hear positive chatter from the infielders. Second and third base, shortstop, first base players should be saying to their pitchers:

- *The batters blind, put that ball in there.*
- *He can't hit; you've got him!*
- *This batter's a bum!*

That's what it takes to win in sports competition, in economic competition and in life. Teams get psyched up and go for the gold. Nobody gets psyched up talking negatively.

Most of the time, what we say is a reflection of what we believe to be true. The most important thing to reemphasize is that **we believe it a lot more after we have said it.**

- *Of all the millions of creatures on earth, a well-developed language is a unique and awesome power available only to the human soul. It's a tremendous power that is usually taken entirely for granted.*
- *So, one of the ways we can control our attitude and our outlook on life is to be careful what we say.*
- *It doesn't happen by accident. It does take mental discipline and lots of it to control our mouths.*

Like other kinds of challenges, we have to recognize our problem, and then we have to assert the will and the discipline to fix it.

Chapter 5 Attitude of the Soul

In this case, we would need to make sure that what we're saying most of the time is something positive. Become known for encouraging other people; it's a great way to be unique.

- *There's always something positive about any situation.*
- *Talk the solutions. Don't talk the problem.*
- *Don't give up on yourself, it will seem like it's not working for quite a while during which time the reordering of your soul is slowly taking place.*
- *Stay with it until one day you will realize a profound shift has taken place in your outlook on life.*

In review, three powerful choices that affect our attitudes are:

1. The information we choose to take into our minds
2. The thoughts that we choose to retain and dwell upon
3. The words that we choose to speak and thus affirm

Our positive attitudes will help bring other people up or our negative attitudes will help bring others down.

- *What we say to other people is important.*
- *Our conversations at work can be a big factor in everyone's morale and employee morale is a significant factor in productivity and business success.*
- *Encourage one another, do not be a discouraging factor in your own life or in the lives of other people.*

It is no accident that only humans have the capability for complex language as it is a spiritual gift that can be used for good or bad. Positive talk is uplifting, it's something that makes those around us feel good and it strengthens our souls and wards off fear.

**It is not food that goes into your mouth that defiles you.
You are defiled by the words that issue from your mouth.**
...Matthew 15:11

A Soul's Code of Conduct

Provide positive feedback. If someone does something well, be positive about it and help that person feel great by recognizing their accomplishment and encouraging him or her.

It is just amazing that we each have the power to make one another feel great, just by sincerely complimenting people who deserve a pat on the back. We have the power to do that every day. How often do you sincerely compliment others?

However, we should only be complimentary of others when they deserve it; otherwise, it soon becomes meaningless.

What would happen to someone who was caught at work putting a couple of drops of poison, say cyanide or strychnine, into everyone's morning coffee each day?

- It would be a serious crime that would not be tolerated.
- They would be fired and criminal charges would be filed against them for attempted murder.
- Yet, some people go around speaking negatively to their friends and co-workers, poisoning everyone's attitude a little at a time, and we think nothing of it.
- Most of the time the negativity is not even recognized for the poison it is.

The bottom line is if you can't say something good, don't say anything at all. Don't have something negative to say about everything someone else says.

It can be very hard to change if negativity is an ingrained habit, but that habit develops into part of your attitude. So, don't be a fuming, negative sorehead with a bad attitude and negative vibes coming out of you like shock waves radiating pessimistic fallout all over everyone else.

"Opportunities multiply as they are seized."
...Ancient Chinese philosopher Sun Tzu

Chapter 5 Attitude of the Soul

You may recall that "emotional contagion" is a process by which people catch the happy, sad, fearful or angry moods of others. The emotional contagion effect can impact your mood very quickly and, over time, it can affect your attitude. Military leaders do not let fearful talk get started among soldiers in combat.

People who tend to be negative or critical often seem to lack dignity or respect for themselves. Instead of **directing** their lives, they just react to their circumstances.

- *For some reason, negative people lead negative, frustrated, problem-filled lives.*
- *They never seem to get over it.*
- *It's just one big problem after the other*
- *For them, life is just one string of continuing hassles.*

Some people constantly bore others with their health problems. Unfortunately, they don't realize that we can talk ourselves into being sicker by constantly verbalizing our illnesses.

- *It's the same principle of believing what you are saying that we mentioned above.*
- *The research conducted by Ms. Pryce-Jones revealed that the happiest most positive employees take 66% less sick leave than the least happy negative employees.*

Just make sure you're not a "Critical Crow" or a "Bad Attitude Bear" that everyone else sees as Mr. or Ms. Negativity, when you could be a positive influence on others who would enjoy being around you.

We should examine our attitudes very carefully, and think with awareness about what we are saying because as human beings we have a hard time recognizing our own faults.

> Whatever you allow to captivate your mind will rule your life.
> ...Gloria Copeland

A Soul's Code of Conduct

If a group had five positive people and five negative ones, and if you asked those with negative attitudes to identify themselves by raising their hands, no one would do so because no one thinks their attitude is negative.

- *Most critical or negative people think they are just "telling it like it is."*
- *If you are negative, the chances are you are the only one who doesn't know it.*

Again, **three ways** we can take control of our own attitudes are:

1. Choose **what to allow into our minds** by what we listen to, watch and read.
2. Choose **what to think about** and retain in our minds.
3. Choose carefully **what we talk about** all day long with other people. Be a positive influence with others.

Attitudes are not developed over night, and they cannot be reformed overnight; therefore, it will take persistence and mental discipline over time to see meaningful change.

The following is a secret taught by Former U.S. Congressman and motivational speaker, Ed Foreman. He explains a unique and fun way to establish and maintain a positive attitude:

We have the choice, when we get up each morning, to choose whether we want to have a day that is good, bad or indifferent.

Of course, very few people would consciously choose to have a bad day or days of indifference.

Therefore, Ed developed a method to help you remember that you've chosen to have a good day every day.

Whenever you are asked how you're doing or someone says, "How are you?" you respond with "Terrific! I am having a terrific day."

The effect of the other person's reaction to that statement as well as the fact that you have once more spoken and **affirmed in your own mind** that you are having a terrific day will surprise you.

Chapter 5 Attitude of the Soul

It will remind you that, hey, you are having a terrific day, especially compared to the billions of sick, poor and otherwise less fortunate people in the world. You should be feeling terrific!

The secret, however, is that you must do it for at least 30 days straight. You must keep doing it, until you've done it so often that it becomes a virtuous habit.

When you start responding with terrific, people will say, "Really, I don't hear that very often." or, "I wish I felt terrific."

We meet people many times each day and usually we all say the same thing: "How're you doing?" In response, most people say, "Fine, how are you?"

However, if somebody says, "How are you?" And the response is "I'm terrific!" They wonder if they have run into a nut or what.

It's interesting to go into stores to the checkout locations where the cashiers talk to hundreds of people a day. While ringing up people's things, they politely ask, "How are you doing today?" And they hear "fine, how are you?" over and over all day long.

*If you respond instead by saying, "I'm having a **terrific** day!"*

They might say with a surprised look, "You are? That's great!"

They too could feel terrific if they just knew the secret.

Of course, you will forget a few times and catch yourself saying, "Fine." Concentrate on it some more until "Terrific" finally becomes an ingrained response.

About the 31st or 32nd day, somebody will say, "Hi, how are you?"

*You will never even have to think about it; "**Terrific**!" will be out of your mouth in a flash, automatically. At that point, you will have mastered one of the most important things you will ever learn about life.*

*It really works, because each time you greet someone you are telling them how great you feel, but more importantly, you are again telling **yourself,** that you are having a terrific day.*

- *If you can get to that point, your outlook on life will begin to*

A Soul's Code of Conduct

improve dramatically.

- *Even if your attitude is good to start with, it can get better.*

Sometimes you feel so bad, that you really don't feel terrific. However, even if you have to reach up there with your hands and make your mouth say terrific, you do it because that's when you need the boost it provides the most! It helps you and everyone around you.

When you no longer have to stop and think about it, when something deep inside of you comes out with "Terrific!" you will know **your soul has made a significant transition.**

The more positive we are, the more we can be in the flow of God's will for us. God is certainly positive, and to flow with him we must be positive as well.[4]

IV. Summary

In review, there are three steps to improving our souls' attitudes for eternity. All three involve our minds because our minds are the battlegrounds where positive and negative thoughts are fighting for control of our souls. Become known for your positive attitude with the following five steps:

1. Take **control of the communications going into your mind** based on what you read, watch and hear.

2. Do not subject yourself to excessive negative or critical influence.

3. Listen to upbeat music, comedy and positive motivational or inspirational and religious material.

4. Take **control over the things that you frequently think about** and dwell on in your mind. Replace stinking thinking with the good stuff; visualize your success.

5. Take **control over the kinds of things you talk about.** Put a guard on your mouth and avoid speaking negatively!

A fool's mouth is his destruction, and his lips are the snare of his soul.
...Proverbs 18:7

Chapter 5 Attitude of the Soul

However, that's just the beginning because you have to stay with it and keep fighting back every time negative critical thought and speech try to reassert themselves.

When asked, "How are you?" respond with "Terrific," for at least 30 days, or until you get in the firm habit of doing so.

It will help you improve your attitude greatly. It will make you a more valuable friend, family member, employee and asset to society. In fact, terrific is the code word for a positive attitude.

At this point, we can summarize the answer to question number five of the most important and enduring human questions of all time.

HOW SHOULD MODERN HUMAN SOULS LIVE?

Each Human Soul should live to attain the most unselfish, positive, faith filled and virtuous character achievable, with the least amount of negativism and the fewest vices possible.

The soul's attitude is a fundamental aspect of its being. Therefore, it must be positive to support the soul's effort to make progress through the challenges of this life.

To be an accepted and respected soul we need to embrace the values, morals and ethics of honorable souls. We do so by replacing selfish thoughts and bad habits with good thoughts and virtuous habits by entering the practices of self-control, faith and prayer.

We should each strive to meet the Divine standards of conduct that have been set before us, while following the Golden Path of Wisdom and Virtue. We can thereby avoid the dozen ever-present Evils of Excess and Devils of Addiction that continue to lead human beings into evil destroying millions of lives in the process every year.

Please remember that the values you hold dear, the thoughts you think, the choices you make, the actions you take, and the friends you make will determine the character of your soul and your eternal destiny.

But those things which proceed out of the mouth, those things come from the soul, and they can defile a man.
...Matthew 15:18

A Soul's Code of Conduct

After winning the last election three years ago, the Socialist took over the federal government and passed legislation prohibiting the sale of all firearms and ammunition. Two years ago, they required gun owners to register all their firearms. Last week, they made it illegal to own guns and began confiscating them. Only government officials, law enforcement and the military will have guns (and the criminals).

Warden's dogs disappeared last night. This morning we found several tranquilizer darts in his yard and the tracks of a large truck in the grass. It has become impossible to find enough dog food to feed all those dogs anyhow, because people have started buying the available dog food for themselves.

Now, I know why Warden has lost more weight than the rest of us: he has been sharing his food with his dogs.

Of course, Warden is really broken up about it, and he falls into a bitter funk thinking about people eating his pets. However, he applies positive thinking discipline because there is too much to do, and he soon pulls out of it. The last thing he ever said about it was, "What a great system Socialism is that it brings us to eating other people's pets."

As more and more doctors have left the country, the lines waiting to get into our compound have lengthened to a quarter mile with most sleeping in their cars along the roadside or living in tents. Doc and the medical staff are nearing exhaustion working twelve and fifteen hours a day to see as many patients as possible. Still patients are waiting in line for three and four days to be seen.

We received a visit from a government official today who gave me a notice stating our clinic is now on the list of designated Federal Health Care Facilities. It also says that henceforth any federal government official who wants medical care is to be seen ahead of those waiting in line because the officials' welfare is more important to the nation than anyone else's.

I protest the unfairness of this and tell them I doubt Doc will agree to do so. They inform me that failure to comply will result in the suspension of Doc's medical license. If we still resist, Doc will be charged with

Chapter 5 Attitude of the Soul

practicing medicine without a license and the clinic will be closed.

Upon hearing this, an exhausted Doc looks out at the long lines of waiting patients and swears he won't go along with it. We decide to think about it and discuss it again in the morning, and of course, Doc goes back to work.

In the morning, we decide to pray about it, and wait to see how many, if any, of these Socialist government officials actually show up for care.

As if to test us, a haughty official shows up the next day demanding to see Doc right away for a very minor problem. As time goes by, the shortage of medical personnel grows worse and the demanding officials begin to show up in increasing numbers, as does the number of regular patients waiting in line.

The injustice of so many pampered bureaucrats cutting in line in front of so many really sick and injured people has become unacceptable, so we decide to set a limit of ten government officials a day and no more. Last week we began enforcing the limit and today, we receive a notice that Doc's medical license has been suspended for disregarding a lawful government order.

This evening the clandestine radio station known as "the resistance" is reporting that restaurants, auto repair stations and numerous other businesses are now required to serve government officials ahead of other people because the official's time is "worth more than anyone else's."

We decide to continue seeing the regular patients still waiting in line for as long as possible, so we shift to an emergency basis. Claire and Doc are working tirelessly, and the nurses have discontinued the paperwork and are treating patients. Doc had already trained Warden and me in first aid, and we administer care to those we can help.

We have been going on like this for a week now, when another edict is delivered from the government. For the benefit of the people, it says, the American Socialist government has decided to deal with the medical shortage by requiring all medical facilities to obtain permission from the Federal Healthcare Assessment Review Board before treating anyone over the age of 65 who is retired and no longer working.

A Soul's Code of Conduct

Doctors will now be required to provide a written health assessment of these older patients so the review board can decide the economic value of their remaining lives. The oldest and sickest patients are the least likely to be approved for any further medical care.

Doc is furious saying the evil of Socialism is ruining the country by turning people against one another and denying care to those who need it most. "By the time this review board responds, many of the elderly without care will have died already," he shouts, "and the rotten socialists know it."

"They can only get away with it because they now have complete control of medical care. *Medicare for None*" is what it should be called because it will be killing off the seniors who had Medicare to start with!" exclaimed our very angry doctor.

The next day we get a call from our friend the famous archeologist, Dr. Jones calling for help from a legendary Inca holy place called Machu Pichu high in the Andes Mountains of Peru. He wants to send a private jet to pick up six of us at a small, nearby airport for an all-expense paid trip to Peru.

As bad as we need a break, it is a tough decision with so many people still needing our help, and the government possibly shutting us down at any time.

The chronicle of Living as a Modern Soul in a Human Body continues with book six, the exciting conclusion of the series, in which, Carter, Warden and Claire learn of ways to make contact with God, what to expect as death approaches and how to die well.

> "Death and life are in the power of the tongue, and
> they who indulge in it shall eat the fruit of it."
> ...Proverbs 18:21

Post Script

Chapter 5 Attitude of the Soul

Attitude of Joy

According to author Charles Swindoll, happiness differs from joy in the sense that happiness comes from the same root word as happening. Happiness is a good feeling based on what is happening to us. Joy on the other hand comes from our soul based on an attitude of godly faith that is less affected by external circumstances.[5]

Previously noted holocaust survivor Viktor Frankl wrote:

"Everything can be taken from a man but one thing: the last of the human freedoms--- to **choose one's attitude** in any given set of circumstances, to choose one's own way."[6]

Swindoll says, "If we pursue happiness instead of choosing joy, we will become as Frankel put it, "playthings of circumstance." Our inner peace will be tossed back and forth according to the will of events beyond our control. But if we exercise our right to **choose our attitude** -- the one basic freedom that can't be taken away from us" -- we can sustain joy even in difficult situations.

When in pursuit of happiness, we need certain things to make us happy; we are dependent on other people, things or circumstances to provide our enjoyment. A happiness dependent on circumstances can disappear when those circumstances change. With a godly attitude, we need nothing tangible to make us happy because we can consistently maintain our own joy in life that won't disappear when needed most.

We can and should aspire to both joy and happiness. One is certain by choice of attitude and faith while the other depends on the management of varying external circumstances.

---

[1] Robert Schwartz, *Your Soul's Plan*, Frog Books, Berkeley, CA P.279
[2] James Allen, *As a Man Thinketh*, DeVorss & Company, Camarillow, CA P.47-48.
[3] Dorothy Hulst, *As a Woman Thinketh*, DeVorss Publications Camarillow, CA, P.42
[4] Joyce Meyer, *Battlefield of the Mind*, Faith Words Hachette Book Group, New York, NY, 2008 p.43
[5] Charles Swindoll, *Laugh Again*, Insight for Living, Anaheim, CA, 1992, p.25
[6] Viktor E. Frankl, *Man's Search for Meaning*, (rev.ed.), NY, NY: Simon & Schuster, Pocket Books, 1984, p. 86.

Appendix 1

The Tabernacle

Claire sees herself outdoors somewhere in a desert location standing in the middle of a very large rectangular space surrounded by high, attractive fabric walls. In the middle of the front half of the enclosure is a large, apparently bronze alter or grill with an offering of some kind of burnt animal on it, and behind the alter is a large bronze washbasin. Situated in the middle of the back half of the enclosure is a smaller rectangular structure with a tent-like covering of smooth animal skins stretched over and across its higher walls

People who appear to be priests are moving about in the enclosure. However, despite her efforts to talk to them, they don't seem able to see or hear her. Hoping she is not a ghost; Claire follows the ornately dressed chief priest into the smaller enclosure and observes him conducting a ritual. Inside she notices a large seven-armed golden candelabra, a table and a smaller grill all covered in gold. The back third of the room is curtained off with a richly colored purple veil.

Eventually the chief priest parts the veil and enters the area behind it with Claire following right behind. To her amazement she sees the famed Ark of the Covenant, a large gold covered chest with a winged cherub on each end of the lid with wings forward facing the center. The location atop the ark between the cherubim was the mercy seat said to be a location for the spirit of God.

Spellbound, Claire realizes she is in the "holy of holies" in the tabernacle, a portable temple used by the Israelites for 400 years from about 1,440 BC until King Solomon built the permanent temple in Jerusalem. Only the high priest was ever allowed in the holy of holies.

The high priest following a ritual cleansing removes two stone tablets and performs some kind of other ritual involving them. Looking at the engraved writing on the tablets, Claire discovers she can actually make out the ancient Hebrew words of the Ten Commandments as if they are in English. She is getting dizzy then falls asleep and awakens back in her room at the base camp with a new understanding of Divine law.

26th U.S. President Theodore Roosevelt said that to educate a person in mind and not in morality is to educate a menace to society.

Appendix 1
Soul's Code of Conduct

Divine Standards of Human Conduct

I. Introduction

The following information offers some guidance to help in understanding the Divine standards for the conduct of human souls and the difference between the more serious and less serious violations of those standards. In addition, summary values and personality traits are briefly discussed.

II. Standards

*There are certain **universal standards of moral conduct** that seem to be true in all places and at all times. For example, murder, rape, theft, and lying and cheating for personal gain have been considered unacceptable, offensive human behaviors in all earthly human societies and cultures.*

The original judgement that these are bad activities had to originate from somewhere outside of our earthly societies since it has affected all human civilizations universally even those in previous times that were isolated geographically from one other.

The source of these "universal moral standards" would be a spiritual cosmic order or creating force that implanted them in the human soul at the dawn of human creation.

Today we are still products of that spiritual cosmic order that we now understand to be God's creation. Most of us feel an inborn duty to honor the Divine standards embedded within our souls, although we have the free will to ignore them and many people do

*As previously noted, it has been reasoned that the very presence of the **universal** moral standards of conduct in so many unrelated human cultures across time is one indicator of God's existence.*

*In some Christian traditions, a **moral** offense is one soul committing offensive acts against itself, against other souls or against Divine law. The sacred sacrament of baptism is said to confer on **repentant** and **willing** souls a state of **divine grace** that includes the benefit of forgiveness for*

Appendix 1
Soul's Code of Conduct

*the lesser moral transgressions of life known as **venial** sins, which humans seem unable to avoid.*

A **Mortal** (deadly) offense, on the other hand, is offensive conduct so serious that it could render a soul unfit for Divine grace.

For an offense to be mortal or deadly to the soul committing it, it must meet **all** of the following three standards at the same time:

1) It must involve a **serious matter** of serious consequence.

2) Before the offense, the soul must have been aware that it was considering a serious wrong, with **sufficient reflection, beforehand.** (Premeditated with Malice Aforethought)

3) A soul must have freely chosen to commit the offense, with the full consent of their own **freewill** (even if encouraged by others).

Below is a list of the most potentially serious moral offenses, which have become the core standards of human moral and ethical conduct in most modern societies.

Some are moral standards involving dishonorable conduct toward other people or God (by abusing the divine nature of your soul). However, they are not necessarily against the criminal law of your society. Others, like murder, are not only moral offenses, but criminal offenses as well because they are against the laws of society.

The difference between a less serious (venial) offense and a very serious (mortal) offense is not always clear and it often depends on the specific circumstances.

The basic meaning of these Divine directives[1] is recorded on the following pages. Each of the them is followed by questions to help you consider if and how you might be violating the standard. Under some circumstances, any of the following examples could be grave enough to rise to the level of a mortal offense if it is seriously considered ahead of time and intentionally committed of one's own free will.

1) Put Nothing Ahead of a Sacred Relationship with God and Worship no Image or idol.

Appendix 1
Soul's Code of Conduct

Do you acknowledge one God who cares about our activity and desires that we take care of his world?
Do you resent the concept of God?
Do you put more faith in astrology, money or luck than in God?
Do you try to communicate with God in prayer?
Do you spend most of your time, attention and resources on things?

According to Pastor and author Kyle Idleman,[2] Idolatry is the most commonly broken of the Ten Divine commandments. The concept being that we allow many of God's gifts such as food, sex, entertainment, money, success, achievement, romance, family or pride in ourselves to become more important than the God who gave them to us.

In so doing, we make false gods or idols of things that are fine and good in themselves, until we elevate them to the essential center of our lives. God loves us so much that he doesn't want to share our main loyalty and allegiance. So, to him this may be idolatry or spiritual adultery.

2) Use Not the Name of God in Vain.
Do you use God's name in reverence only?
Do you use God's name as a curse when angry?
Do you commit Blasphemy (words of Hatred or Defiance towards God)?
Do you seriously slander or insult sacred people or beliefs?

3) Keep the Sabbath Day Holy.
Do you attend church on the Sabbath?
Do you do unnecessary work for pay on Sunday?[3]
Do you require employees to work on Sundays in non-essential occupations?

4) Love and Respect Your Parents and Your Children.
Do you love, help, and obey your parents?
Do you seriously care for your aged parents?
Do you see to the proper moral education of your children?
Do you physically or mentally abuse or seriously neglect your parents or children?
Do you disobey or disrespect those in authority over you?

Appendix 1
Soul's Code of Conduct

5) Do Not Murder.

Have you murdered or seriously harmed anyone?
Have you seriously entertained thoughts of suicide?
Do you take or sell dangerous illegal drugs?
Have you promoted, committed or had an Abortion?
Are you guilty of animal abuse and cruelty?

6) Do Not Commit Adultery.

Do you commit adultery or sexual immorality (having any kind of sex with anyone other than a spouse)?
Sexuality is the fountain of life, so when abused it is said to be debasing and destructive of the human soul.[4]

7) Do Not Steal.

Do you steal money, or the property of others?
Have you defrauded workers of their just wages?
Have you stolen your employer's time, by doing less than your best at what you are paid to do?
Have you inflated your expenses or travel account?
Are you guilty of fraud or stealing money from an employer (embezzlement)?
Have you received, concealed, bought or sold stolen property?
Have you willfully defaced or destroyed another's property?
Have you gambled with resources needed by your family?
Have you not repaid loans?
Have you pirated computer software, or bootlegged movies or DVDs or violated copyright laws?
Have you evaded or cheated on your tax return?

8) Do Not Lie to or About Other People.

Do you tell serious or premeditated lies?
Do you gossip about or exaggerate other people's faults?
Have you violated the confidence of someone without reason?
Have you given false testimony?

9) Seek Not More Than You Earn nor Covet the Property of Others.

Appendix 1
Soul's Code of Conduct

Are you greedy?
Do you seriously seek after someone else's possessions?

III. Grace

In Christian denominations, it is understood that God is a spirit of pure, holy, **uncontaminated love** who wants all of us to come into a holy, loving fellowship with Him because, by definition, **love requires relationships**. For that to be possible, we also have to become holy and uncontaminated with sin. Since we cannot seem to live holy lives on our own, God has arranged for us to be made clean by his forgiveness through the imputation[1] of our sin to His only son.

That forgiving grace could only be extended to humanity through the human incarnation, life, death and resurrection of Jesus Christ. Therefore, to receive God's grace, we must simply **recognize Christ** who made the sacrifice to extend that grace to us and request it through him. That precious, holy grace is thereby free to all who request it, but it is available only in this way.

Since we cannot live a virtuous life, sinless enough to earn God's grace, why try so hard to do so? True Christians aren't trying to live Godly lives to get saved, we try to live Godly lives **because we are saved**. The **sure sign** that people have accepted and been saved by God's grace is that they are doing their **very best** to live a Godly life. If not, their behavior betrays the fact that they are rejecting God's offer with contempt and demonstrating that they believe they don't need God or his grace and are not interested in fellowship with Him now, or in the life to come.

Because God is love, he hates the concept of hell more than we do. It is against all that He stands for. Sadly, however, it is the destination of the souls who continue to reject God's offer of grace thus condemning themselves to a place completely beyond the protection of God's holy presence.

> **"We are created to worship God, love people and use things.**
> **Too often we use people, love self and worship things."**
> ...*Theologian Dr. David Jeremiah*

---

[1] *See book six Chapter 3*

Appendix 1
Soul's Code of Conduct

*In some religious traditions, one can be **restored** to a state of grace following a mortal offense through a process of penance that involves four steps:*

1. *Confession - acknowledgement of your offense*
2. *Contrition - true regret for your actions*
3. *Forgiveness - asking forgiveness for your offense*
4. *Satisfaction - a physical, financial or other sacrifice made for breaking Divine law such as fasting, donations to charity etc.*

Even when God forgives our offenses, their previous destructive impact upon our bodies may yet endure.

IV. Christian Virtues and Vices

Spiritual virtues according to Galatians 5:19:

1. **Love** - the power that moves us to respond to someone's needs with no expectation of reward.
2. **Joy** - An inward hope and exuberance in spite of outward circumstances
3. **Peace** - A supernatural calm amid chaos and the ability to bring harmony to divided factions
4. **Forbearance** - the quiet willingness to accept irritating or painful situations
5. **Kindness** - generosity and consideration of others
6. **Goodness** - moral excellence
7. **Faithfulness** - enduring loyalty and trustworthiness
8. **Gentleness** - the power to control your reactions to difficult people and situations
9. **Self-control** - the ability to restrain inappropriate passions and appetites

Sinful vices according to Galatians 5:19-21 include:

1. **Sexual immorality** – adultery, homosexuality, fornication
2. **Impurity** – unwholesomeness, uncleanliness or contamination
3. **Debauchery** – wickedness, corruption or dishonesty
4. **Idolatry** – worship and adoration of something other than God

Appendix 1
Soul's Code of Conduct

5. **Witchcraft** – *occultism, sorcery, spiritually evil activities*
6. **Hatred** – *intense dislike, ill will, disgust or bitter opposition*
7. **Discord** – *disharmony, conflict, strife and disagreement*
8. **Jealousy** – *suspicious distrust and anxiety about rivals, envy*
9. **Fits of rage** – *uncontrolled, furious, angry, or violent outbreaks*
10. **Selfish ambition** – *strong desire to achieve only for oneself*
11. **Dissensions and Factions** – *people divided against one another*
12. **Drunkenness** – *incapacity from alcoholic intoxication*
13. **Orgies** – *parties associated with intoxication and sexual immorality.*

V. Values and Personality in Moral Psychology

In the field of Moral Psychology, the following ten values are often considered as universal because they are held in varying degree by people of most cultures. Our values affect our behavior, and these general values could encompass and represent the many other more detailed moral values previously noted in this series.[5]

1. **Power** - *being in a position of authority or control*
2. **Security** - *safety, stability, harmony and order*
3. **Self-direction** - *being free to make your own decisions in life*
4. **Hedonism** - *freedom for self-indulgent pleasure seeking*
5. **Tradition** - *respect for the customs and beliefs of your culture*
6. **Achievement** - *valuing the accomplishment of significant goals*
7. **Conformity** - *respecting social norms and not offending people*
8. **Stimulation** - *pursuit of challenging and exciting activities*
9. **Benevolence** - *caring for and about people you know*
10. **Universalism** - *care about humanity and nature in general.*

Even people with the same values, may react differently to the same situation because they prioritize their values differently.

Most of Modern man's health problems come from trying to feed the soul with food meant for the body.
...*Author Frank Farrell*

Appendix 1
Soul's Code of Conduct

Personality *refers to a person's earthly patterns of thinking, feeling and behaving due to* ***influences*** *of body, soul and culture. Our* ***spiritual character is a strong component of earthly personality.***

The field of psychology has developed the following list of the six most important ***personality traits*** *that affect the behavior of human beings:*[6]

1. **Extraversion**- the degree to which one is outgoing and sociable
2. **Neuroticism**- degree of emotional stability
3. **Agreeableness**- degree of positive orientation toward others
4. **Conscientiousness**-degree of responsibility and dependability
5. **Openness**- degree of openness to new experiences and ideas
6. **Honesty-Humility**- degree of honesty, fairness and humility

Although, negative personality traits can influence our behavior and our character, they can be overcome with focused, intentional effort. Therefore, we should be alert to recognize and combat any negative traits in our personalities.

For example, people unusually low in personality trait number six could tend to be selfish, deceitful, manipulative, greedy or sly. This would make it an essential challenge for them to work hard to overcome that negative personality trait and to strengthen their spiritual character in honesty and humility.

> "You have a life story unfolding here and you are the primary author as well as the main character."
> ...Price Pritchett, The Unfolding

---

[1] The Ten Commandments

[2] Kyle Idleman, Gods at War by, Zondervan, Grand Rapids Michigan, 2013

[3] Some faiths consider Saturday as the Sabbath.

[4] The traditional laws said to have been enumerated to Adam, Noah and Moses. These laws also instruct us to establish fair courts of law to dispense justice in the world and to respect all life causing no undue pain.

[5] Professor Mark Leary, Why You Are Who You Are, The Teaching Company, Chantilly VA 2018 Course 1648 Guidebook p.78

[6] Ibid p.11-20

Appendix 2 Self-control

The Art of Self-Control

As has been said, self-control is the door to heaven. To obtain Divine peace, contentment and wisdom, mankind must overcome selfish tendencies and unpleasant emotional passions. This can be accomplished by learning the art of greater self-control. This is not a vague, mystical concept but a very real and practical mental strategy that requires will-power, down to earth dedication and perseverance.

Mastering the art of self-control will take a very serious commitment to pursue it relentlessly so as to change from **vices** to **virtues** habits ingrained from birth or before. One might say selfishness is in our DNA, so mastering this strategy of self-control is a very important process.

The strategy is an orderly progression of overcoming vice, corrupt passions and habits of bad conduct through five stages, which philosopher James Allen terms:[1]

1. Repression
2. Endurance
3. Elimination
4. Understanding
5. Victory

It is critical to understand that we must proceed through the five stages in numerical order if we are to find any degree of success in the end. Just as we cannot expect a fireplace to produce heat before we provide it with wood.

1. The first stage is **Repression**, which involves repressing misconduct before it is acted out. Stifling, for instance, angry responses, insulting comments or other unkind words or actions including temptations to gluttony, adultery, and all of the other vices.

It takes great effort not to return anger for anger and to smother our natural instincts to defend and justify ourselves. Expect it to be painful and difficult at first. Nevertheless, it can be done, and with continued practice we can begin to succeed more and more often until at last we can successfully choke off our reactions to temptation and antagonism before we can act them out.

2. At this point we can progress to the second stage of **Endurance** wherein we must quietly endure the aching resentment that arises in our minds at the offensive acts of others, the relentless pull of our addictions or our failure to do what we should to be successful in life. In this stage we must realize that our distress is arising from our own weakness and that giving in to it is exactly the wrong response. Furthermore, it is these challenges and temptations that are illuminating our weaknesses precisely so that we may conquer them.

3. From the first two difficult stages, we move to the third stage of **Elimination**, in which we focus on **preventing the wrong thoughts and impulses that** provoke bad activity in the first place. Once accomplished, this preempts the distress of the previous two stages, which is replaced with a sense of conscious control, a feeling akin to holy joy and a much calmer mind.

4. This state leads to the fourth stage of **Understanding** and deeper insight into the beginning, development and manifestation of sin, iniquity and failure in our lives. A true understanding of this mental corruption should lead to complete self-control. It then becomes impossible for the seeds of corruption and failure to infect our now forearmed minds and ripen to malicious thoughts, acts and consequences.

5. In the final stage of **Victory**, the antagonism of others, challenges and temptations no longer trouble our minds. Therefore, in full self-control, we are able to wisely enjoy life and steer ourselves on a course to more success, peace and happiness.

"Get yourself off of your mind"
...Bishop E.W. Jackson

---

[1] Allen, James, *Above Life's Turmoil,* Lexington: WLC Books, 2009 p.51

In Mark 7:20, the Messiah explains that it is not what or how we eat that makes us unclean. It is our vile thoughts, words and deeds that contaminate us.

He says, it is what comes out of a person that defiles them for it is from within, out of a person's heart that evil thoughts come ---- sexual immorality, theft, murder, adultery, greed, malice, deceit, lewdness, envy, slander, arrogance and folly. All these evils originate from inside and thereby defile a person's soul.

**Whatever is true, honorable, right, pure, lovely, of good repute
and excellence, and worthy of praise
dwell on these things.**
...Phil. 4:8

Author Biography

Author
James L. Cannon
Lt. Colonel U.S. Army (Ret.)

Mr. Cannon is a retired university vice president, a former economics professor and a former corporate manager.

Lt.Col. Cannon is a Vietnam War veteran. He has been an undercover intelligence operative, and he retired as a decorated Army Reserve Intelligence Officer with the Defense Intelligence Agency in Washington, D.C.

As a community leader, the author has been a successful small city mayor; a chamber of commerce president and has served on the governing boards of several public organizations.

The Colonel holds University of Virginia degrees in economics and foreign affairs; GTE marketing, management and technology degrees and is an honor graduate of the U.S. Army's Command and General Staff College and a graduate of the University of Kentucky College Business Management Institute.

The author is happily married with a beautiful wife, two children, two grandchildren, a dog and a small business. His interests include metaphysics, economics and philosophy.

The author may be contacted by email at soulsline9@gmail.com

Made in the USA
Columbia, SC
09 July 2023